D0124839

Effective Small Churches
in the Twenty-first Century

Effective Small Churches in the Twenty-first Century

Carl S. Dudley

Abingdon Press

Nashville

EFFECTIVE SMALL CHURCHES IN THE TWENTY-FIRST CENTURY—
A Revised and Updated Edition of *Making the Small Church Effective*

Library of Congress Cataloging-in-Publication Data

Dudley, Carl S., 1932-
    Effective small churches in the twenty-first century / Carl S.
Dudley.—[Rev. ed.].
        p. cm.
    Rev. ed. of: Making the small church effective. 1978.
    Includes bibliographical references and index.
    ISBN 0-687-09090-3 (pbk. : alk. paper)
    1. Small churches. I. Dudley, Carl S., 1932-Making the small church
effective. II. Title.

BV637.8 .D825 2003
254—dc21

2002154149

03 04 05 06 07 08 09 10 11 12—10 9 8 7 6 5 4 3 2 1
MANUFACTURED IN THE UNITED STATES OF AMERICA

Contents

PART TWO: BELONGING

PART THREE: SHARING

Introduction: Effective Small Churches in the Twenty-first Century

By all odds, small churches should have died in the past quarter century. They remind me of the old-timer who was asked if he had lived in that area all his life. "Nope," he said with a wiry smile, "not yet. But I intend to."

Small churches have a will to live—against all odds. Consider the forces allied against small church success. The phenomenal growth of their opposite, the megachurches of several thousand members, have dominated the religious landscape. Judging from reports in news media, it is hard to imagine that anyone was left to join small churches. At the same time, denominational organizations, once central to small-church identity, have declined in total members, financial support, and influence, reducing a once crucial lifeline of aid and encouragement.[1] Minimum salaries for clergy have increased at the same time that supplemental aid for denominations has declined. Social mobility has hurt the small church since family continuity is broken when young people leave the communities of their youth to seek additional educational and employment opportunities, and older members retire in distant places or self-contained retirement homes. Traditional family life, once the backbone of small-church social networks, has been undermined by both parents being employed, rising divorce rates, single parent homes, blended families, and multiple locations that children call home.

Beyond structural changes in church and in family life, the small church has been hit by a radical shift in values that challenge every congregation, regardless of size. Baby boomers (born 1945–1965) have proven much less interested than their parents in joining churches, an all too familiar generational pattern of values that rejects many traditional institutions, including, but not limited to, churches. Generation Xers (born 1965–1985) have only escalated the alienation. Small church intimacy and relational character create unique barriers when they seek to embrace the boomers and Xers within a tight-knit congregational family. When you ask the elderly leaders of old, mainline congregations where their children worship, you are most apt to hear that "they are good kids, and spiritual—just not particularly religious." This generally means they don't attend church anywhere anymore. The younger generations' emphasis on a personal spiritual journey would seem out of character with small churches. The younger generations' music, designed to challenge existing standards, would seem offensive to the deep roots of small-church traditions.

Remarkably, in spite of all these competitive forces, small churches have survived. Even though challenged by significant obstacles, their relative strength has not declined in the past quarter century. In 1975, we found that in mainline denominations, the smallest 50 percent of churches served about 15 percent of the members, and conversely, the largest 15 percent of the churches served 50 percent of the members.[2] The same distribution of membership was reported among mainline denominations in 2000. Small churches are not just surviving; numerically they are the majority. In the Faith Communities Today (FACT) Report, the largest and most inclusive study of faith communities in the United States,[3] half of the congregations have less than one hundred Regularly Participating Adults (RPA, see Fig. 1). This book is written in appreciation of these churches.

A quarter century ago, Abingdon Press published my experiences with small congregations under the title *Making the Small Church Effective* (Nashville: Abingdon Press, 1978). Since then, I have been in conversation with countless pastors and church leaders for whom the book has served as a "mini-survival kit for small-church ministry." Although their stories of people are sometimes tough and tragic, their personal relationships are real and lasting. Typically they conclude with a wistful comment about how much they loved, and were loved by, the congregation. "But," they add, "times are changing."

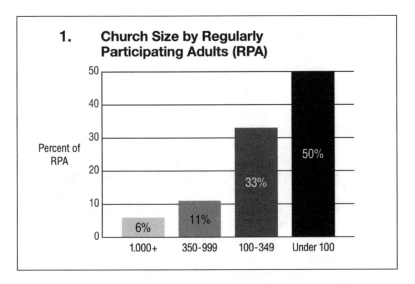

1.   Church Size by Regularly Participating Adults (RPA)

Faith Communities Today (FACT) data of 14,301 congregations show half have under 100 Regularly Participating Adults (RPA).

This is a book about continuity in the midst of change. When Abingdon editor Bob Ratcliff encouraged revision of the earlier text for a new generation of leaders, I became more acutely aware of the diverse and deep forces of change in twenty-five years. At the same time, so many conversations with small-church leaders convinced me that small churches continue to make foundational and sometimes radical contributions of embodied faith in their communities. The initial thesis of the book remains: small churches are not organizational errors to be corrected, but intentional choices of members who put a priority on human relationships. The task of small-church leaders is to maximize their potential impact with a remarkable array of resources that they use intuitively.

Against the onslaught of negative forces, many of these churches are doing well. Our task is not to tell small churches how to minister, but to help leaders identify and celebrate what they are doing well, and to encourage them to claim this ministry as their own. In the process, we can see how the basic relational power of small churches has been enhanced by several new developments in the past quarter century. These resources and approaches should be identified and intentionally incorporated to strengthen small church ministry.

Social Capital

With surprising enthusiasm, the larger community has discovered the "secret" of the small congregation—that face-to-face communication is absolutely foundational for developing personal character and community trust at every level of the society. Although the importance of social capital is no surprise to small churches, the discovery has provided an amazing array of analytical tools, interested academics, and favorable conditions for the kinds of things small churches do best—although the specific materials they produce are not always directly applicable to small churches.

Congregational Awareness

Although academic disciplines previously recognized that congregations had "character" (as have many subcultures in society), recent materials have especially emphasized the unique culture of each congregation. The development of a new, multidisciplinary approach commonly called "congregational studies" has greatly expanded the toolbox of analytical instruments that leaders can use to better understand and mobilize the energies of churches of all sizes. Congregational studies provide lenses for seeing the church's social context, leadership, resources, culture, theology, and other dimensions that contribute to a particular congregational identity. Threatened by socially divisive forces, small-church leaders appreciate resources to strengthen a congregational sense of belonging, purpose, and unity.

Religious Capital

As leaders became more attentive to the voices and rituals of small-membership churches, congregations discovered the depth of faith that they embody in who they are and how they live. Through congregational studies, especially, but not exclusively, in small churches, social analysts began talking like theologians about the faith they found in the patterns of social interaction and corporate behavior. In this conversation, "practical theology" was redefined as the "practice of theology," as finding belief in action more than explaining beliefs in abstractions. This expression of lived-faith has been observed and described in a full range of behavior from liturgical worship to habits of daily life. When challenged by a new generation that has privatized the search for God, small churches need to share a faith that is immanently practical and portable for those who understand themselves on a spiritual journey.

Small Church Materials

In contrast to the mid-1970s, when few publications were available, materials for small churches are plentiful in virtually every aspect of ministry. The small church has become a popular focus for study and writing, providing excellent materials in worship and preaching, in evangelism and education, in spiritual retreats and social outreach, and in vision and renewal. Existing literature in the 1970s typically defined small churches as a problem to be solved, a seed to be grown, or a miniature organization that needed to be filled out with more people. Most of the current materials have affirmed and enriched the foundational concept of relationships (with God and among members) as the primary strength of small congregations. The variety and focused character of these publications allows leaders to find helpful program materials that address the issues of particular concern in their own congregation. I have used extended endnotes to retain the best of the past and incorporate new materials, and in each chapter I recommend the most helpful materials in "Suggestions for Further Reading."

Electronic Communications

Since Samuel F. B. Morse developed his first "telegraphic device" in 1837, we have been a society with increasingly complex and useful electronic communications, especially in the last quarter century, and there is no reason to believe that the end is in sight. Telephone, television, fax machines, copy machines, computers, email and web sites have all impacted the small church in positive as well as negative ways. We must approach this with care, since the financial and educational investment necessary to enter and maintain electronic networks has marginalized populations that are already disadvantaged. But for a relational community, these devices seem a natural way to keep people in the loop even when they are thousands of miles apart or have only limited time for conversation.

Niche Marketing

"Diversity" is a label that covers massive social changes that have penetrated into communities throughout the country. The immigrant experience of New York City impacts the entire nation—towns in central Iowa may have a community of Thai residents competing for local factory jobs, and a Texas community has a colony of Vietnamese fishing families expecting education for their children. These immigrants bring their faith communities, transforming the religious landscape with choices that are essential to them and appealing to others. At the same time, the boomers and Xers revel in a world of choices, in education and employment, in sexual orientation and lifestyle, in marriage and family arrangements, in arts, music, and recreation. From both within the old Christian ethos and from the presence of new cultural choices, diversity or pluralism is a central fact of the new millennium. For small churches, this suggests a new kind of intentionality in ministry that is clear in identity and pro-active in seeking its appropriate participant groups. Christians, in particular, can no longer assume that everyone knows who they are and for what they stand. Small churches are uniquely positioned in a competitive niche market to define themselves and find their own people—which, in a racially segregated world, can be "multicultural in Christ." Building on the storehouse of tradition, they can choose not a fateful repetition of the past, but a coherent Christian vision for a spiritually hungry world.

New Networks

Declining denominational structures may seem a natural consequence to all that we have noted above. As denominational income shrinks, the capacity to aid small churches has, of necessity, been scaled back. At the same time, many small congregations that never felt particularly close to the denominational agencies still continue to celebrate their religious, ethnic, and cultural heritage. Most of the liturgy, rituals, and habits of denominational traditions seem firmly in place, even as their organizational structures are shrinking. Further, small churches seem amazingly agile in their capacity to join existing networks and form new alliances for the tasks they feel are essential to ministry. They appear to move with relative ease into partnerships with local groups, often composed of church members or their families, friends, and business associates. In the past quarter century, we have seen a radical dissolution of the "walls" that once separated church and state into far more fluid relationships between faith-based groups, government agencies, educational institutions, and philanthropic organizations. For small churches, these separations were always more personal, never so contained by legal definitions. Organizationally, even as denominations decline, local congregations seem remarkably positioned and prepared to deal creatively with cultural change.

For all these reasons, community building in small congregations has changed since the publication of *Making the Small Church Effective* in 1978. By agreement with the publisher, the format of the earlier book will remain, with revisions that reflect strategies to adapt to new conditions. While building on the initial sources of our work, I will suggest new resources in the literature for small churches in developing social capital, congregational culture, faith-practices, niche identity, electronic communities, and network strategies. I will show trends and comparisons from Faith Communities Today (FACT), a survey by the Hartford Institute for Religion Research that gathered information on 14,301 congregations in the spring of 2000. Forty-one denominational faith groups participated in the study, including mainline, evangelical and non-denominational Protestants, historically black churches, Roman Catholics, Orthodox Christians, Jews, Mormons, Muslims, Baha'is, and Unitarian-Universalists.[4]

One challenging trend of the 1970s continues: the large congregations become larger, while small churches remain more numerous. Small churches often appear even more inadequate when they are compared to the super-successful megachurches. This disparity is often amplified through megachurch media ministries and distribution networks. In his overview of postmodern

America, Albert Borgmann has suggested two opposite responses to the excesses of modernity: hyperactivity and sullen recognition.[5] We see these responses embodied in these two opposite expressions of faith in our time: the hyperactivity of many megachurches and the sullen atmosphere of many smaller congregations. But the sullen attitude of small churches need not prevail. In reconsidering these ministries, we can incorporate strategies to make the most of their assets among communities of faith.

In the face of radical cultural changes of racial and ethnic composition, generational values, and technological advancements, we engage small-church leaders to maximize their special assets. The strength of small churches remains the priority commitment that members place on their relationships—with each other, with their place, with their history, and with their sense of God's presence that permeates everything they do.

Appreciation

In addition to those congregations and individuals noted in the initial work on which we are building, I want to thank my colleagues in the Hartford Institute for Religion Research and in Faith Communities Today, especially Mart Bailey, Dirk Hart, and David Roozen for extensive comments. Many thanks for specialized and helpful contributions by Ben Helmer, Steve Blackburn, Tony Pappas, Mary Jane Ross, Craig This, Scott Thumma, Sheryl Wiggins, and my friend, companion, and wife, Shirley Dudley. Thanks to my patient and encouraging editor, Bob Ratcliff, and to those pastors and small churches that have shared their ministries with me to provide the basis for this new publication. I thank God for the opportunity to know these people in ministry.

Introduction from
Making the Small Church Effective
(1978, revised)

The basic difference between small churches and larger congregations exists in the human relationships among those who attend. I do not mean that numbers are illusions. Small churches struggle for membership, for money, and for survival. The battle is decided, not by a change of program, but by personal feelings among those who choose to join. Church membership size is not the cause of their problems. It is the result of their values, beliefs, and personal choices.

People who attend small churches give many reasons. Some share the beliefs of the church, some find that group of people especially attractive. Others have a habitual response to the rhythm of the week and the cycle of the seasons. Some have denied that they have made a conscious choice: they say, "This has always been our church." Many of these same people have chosen larger associations for the other dimensions of their lives. They find employment in larger groups, shop in larger centers, send their children to area-wide or consolidated schools, and travel by mass transit. Most could have chosen a larger congregation with very little additional effort. The choice to attend no church is always an option.

This is a book about the people who have *chosen* to belong to small congregations. In 1978, it grew from workshops with pastors and members of small congregations, along with denominational leaders from a broad range of Christian churches: Baptist, Christian (Disciples), Episcopal, Evangelical Covenant, Lutheran,

Mennonite, Presbyterian, Reformed, Roman Catholic, and United Church of Christ. Since then, the material has been shared with congregations in other faith groups, including Independent and Charismatic Christians, Muslim mosques, Jewish synagogues, Baha'i assembly. The book offers resources for understanding and exercises for developing the strengths of belonging in a wide variety of small-membership congregations.

Background

My own motives for working with the small church grew from unresolved tensions within me, which I found reflected in much of the literature about small churches. On one side, we affirm that "small is beautiful." On the other side, we urge membership growth for institutional "success." But if churches grow, then they cease to be small and "beautiful." My own experience reflects this confusion.

On the positive side, I attended a small neighborhood church, even though our family belonged to Old First Church in the center of the city. One summer, when I worked on a farm, I shared with the families of that valley in the experience of the crossroads church. As a student, I served in a suburban new church development. As a seminary intern with my bride, we set up housekeeping in the manse of a yoked parish of three churches in mountain mining communities. In each of these experiences, I found myself in the care of a large "family" called (by outsiders) a "small church." Later in the congestion of the city, I found many of these same family feelings in the urban ethnic and racial parishes. Below the level of consciousness, the affections and afflictions of these small churches have been absorbed into my being.

The other side of my experience with small churches is not as pleasant. After ordination to the gospel ministry, I was asked to serve on a committee of our denomination that had the responsibility for dispersing supplementary funds to "struggling churches." With great diligence I reviewed the mission statements that these small churches presented to the committee. I listened to the stories of their past and their plans for the coming year. I was impressed by the sincerity of their intention to recruit new members. They were committed to being self-sufficient "within three years, four years at the most." The first year I served on this committee, I was deeply impressed. And the second. By the third year, I began to have doubts.

I had been warned. Other members of the committee had often explained the small church in very negative language. They said that small churches were "disorganized, uncommitted, and afraid of change." The most sympathetic members of the committee suggested that small churches are "trapped in their circumstances." The more cynical members confided their considered opinion that small churches are "small of vision," and "limited in leadership." Since I had spent many satisfying years in small congregations, this information was a denial of my personal experience. Their analysis challenged the validity of my experience.

This tension continued for several years. The perennial speeches from church representatives and from committee members became as predictable as if they had been written in a script. The struggling churches needed financial aid each year, "for a little while more." The members of the committee blamed the neighborhood surrounding the church and urged renewed dedication of the leaders. The meeting became an annual ritual. Neither party understood the other, and both disliked what they found themselves doing.

This book is designed to break into that cycle of ecclesiastical condescension and dependency. We do not offer programs that have been borrowed from the ways of larger congregations. We do not retell the success stories of those few high-energy churches that attract a sort of supercharged people from a wide area, but have so little in common with the struggling small church on the corner. We are offering more than sociological analysis, ecclesiastical statistics, and theological purity. Rather we highlight the unique gifts of ministry that are the natural strength of belonging to a small congregation.

In two decades after my ordination, I felt the love of two congregations as their pastor. Throughout my ministry, I have experienced a continuing relationship with perhaps a dozen other congregations, and I have worked with many more congregations intensely, but briefly. From these, I draw the collected personal memories that inform these pages.

Fortunately, I have been able to share with a great many more congregations in the development of the Small-Church Workshop. Through Doctor of Ministry programs in Chicago, Illinois, and Hartford, Connecticut, I have been able to work with several hundred active pastors in a great variety of congregations. These pastors have critically tested, refined, and reported the effect of these resources in ministry with their congregations. As a teacher, conference leader and consultant, I have shared these materials with members and pastors from several thousand congregations in Congregational Studies Institutes, Small-Church Workshops, denominational and regional training events drawn from a wide spectrum of religious congregations, from every section of the country, and from every segment of community life. Participants have enthusiastically tested the approach, reacting and reshaping the tools for their own use and our further edification. The results are surprising, discouraging, and ultimately very hopeful.

Findings

We were genuinely surprised at the basic similarities among all small churches. Of course, we found many differences based on denominational background and demographic situation. Of course, no two churches are ever identical. But in the way that people related to one another, small congregations have more in common with other small churches than they do with larger congregations in the community, or in their denominational communion.

At the same time, we were discouraged in our search for programmatic answers to small-church problems. Belonging to a small church is especially attractive and uniquely satisfying to some people. Program approaches that fit in more "successful" churches often appear self-defeating among people who have chosen to belong to a small church. We cannot assume that affirming the strength of smallness must lead to church membership growth.

Beyond the disappointment of the participants at not finding "an answer" to the problems of the small church, they found the workshops ultimately reassuring. The sessions affirmed the internal strength of the small church. It is the oldest form of Christian witness, and the most numerous expression of every religious body. It has endured, and it is a very durable form to carry the faith in future. It may not have the visibility of massive numbers, or the clout of great capital resources. But neither should it be a drain on the ecclesiastical welfare of the declining denominational largess. The small church has a partnership to play in the religious ecology of the larger society.

The workshops were based on support of small congregations, typically Protestant forms of Christian faith. Most of the feedback came from pastors who feel called to the small church and wish they could remain—but they also have problems. In effect, this book is not a reflection of the problems, but rather it is a reflection of the way the small church is seen by pastors and lay leaders who love it. That makes a difference.

Appreciation

In the preparation of this book, I wish to express my special thanks to several exceedingly honest and very different critics who read the manuscript in its original form, and offered extensive and insightful comments: Margaret S. Boulden, C. Eugene Bryant, Walter G. Cornett III, Theodore H. Erickson, Lyle E. Schaller, Lincoln Richardson, and Shirley A. Wooden. Thanks also to Shirley, my wife and companion, whose steady support and sparkling insight make work into fun. Finally, thanks to the people who have shown me the meaning of Christian ministry— those who have shared their ideas in many workshops across the country, and especially those loving people with whom we shared in pastoral ministry in First Presbyterian Church of Buffalo, New York, and in Berea Presbyterian Church of St. Louis, Missouri.

CHAPTER ONE
Perspectives on the Small Church

What is a small church? Numerical definitions can be mislead-ing, since they obscure the unique character of social dynamics in small churches.

If we think of a continuum of churches that range from small to medium to large, then small churches should be congregations with the lowest one-third of members (or attendance). But there is something quite mysterious and irrational about the working definition of a small church. More than one church executive has explained with a straight face, "Two-thirds of our churches are small." When I ask if that means "two-thirds are below average," they say, "Yes," and then smile at their own impossible math—how can two-thirds be below average?

In practice, the "small church" is too often defined as deficient. Too often the term means that the congregation does not have resources to achieve a standard goal. Those congregations with fewer members are usually less able to generate the human, material, and financial resources to retain an ordained resident pastor and support a full program of church activities. Reduced to a single word, *money* becomes a frequent criterion in defining the small church. In my opinion, this is not a helpful definition, but it is a very common one.

In describing the Episcopal Church, the Reverend James E. Lowrey has used such a practical definition: since 125 pledging units, or at least 250 average communicants, are necessary to gen-erate the resources for a minimum church program, the small church may be defined as those congregations with 250 or fewer communicant members.[1] On this basis, Lowrey continues,

"Forty-three percent of the clergy are serving 18 percent of the people in 62 percent of the parishes in a situation which is programmed for failure." This profile is typical of mainline Protestant churches.

Lyle E. Schaller has maintained that average Sunday attendance is a much more accurate index of basic church membership. He recommends that Protestant churches averaging fewer than forty-five members a Sunday should be classified as small.[2] Congregations above that figure should take heart that they are not small when compared with others. However, Schaller also notes that the "ideal size" for a congregation with one pastor would be about 175 average Sunday attendance.[3] Anything less would have to be considered less than ideal. (Schaller places the figure at 150 average Sunday attendance for a two-church parish, at 125 for a three-church parish.) The break-even number between 45 and 175 average Sunday attendance would depend upon the capacity of the congregation to raise money, and the expectations of the pastor and congregation for adequacy of program activities.

"Small church" is defined on a sliding scale. Within each denominational family, the definition of a small church is based on the expectations of its members. A Mennonite congregation of 75 adult members, for example, would be considered a strong church, while the same number of communicants in a Presbyterian church would rarely be able to attract a clergyperson, or keep a building open for worship and programs. At the most basic level, financial stability is the bottom line for both denominations. Definitions of size depend on access to the funding that each congregation feels is "essential," beyond survival, to provide effective ministry.

The attitudes of the leadership and membership have a determinative effect upon the possibilities for a particular church. "When our perception of reality falls below what really is, . . . we will tend to make modest plans. . . . The lower our self-esteem, the more likely it is that we will concentrate on 'our problems' and on institutional survival rather than on the potentialities for ministry."[4] Since most Protestant churches are financially struggling, we sometimes hear the mathematical confusion; as one executive told me, "The majority of our churches are below average, but they are everywhere."

Small churches are found in every kind of community—city, suburb, and rural village; they are rich and poor and exist in every kind of cultural background. The rural small church is the unmoved image of serenity in the midst of mobile America: in summer, the crossroads church under the spreading shade tree; and in winter, at the heart of the Christmas season, surrounded by driven snow and issuing a warm "Season's Greetings!" Small churches are equally ubiquitous in the urban areas. Including the storefront churches with their many tongues and languages, small churches embrace more people in the congested cities than in the scattered witness of our rural areas. Even in affluent suburban neighborhoods, small churches can be found. They are the "new start congregations" that never grew. They are the small, intentional fellowships, issue-oriented, and without walls. Small churches have taken root everywhere.

They remain, even while everything else is changing. Small churches are tenacious. Some would call them tough. They do not give up when faced with impossible problems. Neither do they experience rapid shifts of membership. Over the years, some may grow and others decline. But they are peculiarly resistant to programmed intervention from outside sources. Million-dollar programs for membership recruitment leave them relatively unaffected. In membership participation, the majority of small churches have not varied 10 percent in any given decade.

At the same time, they will not die. Often financially starved, frequently without a pastor, sometimes deprived of denominational contact or intentionally independent from outside connections, the small congregation will persevere. Many members will resist the rational proposals to "save our church" through moving, merging, yoking, or teaming. The members have faith that they can hold on "somehow." In the words of one frustrated denominational executive, "Small churches are the toughest: they won't grow and they won't go away."

Although the majority of churches are small, the majority of church members belong to larger congregations. Not everyone is attracted to small churches. They may be ubiquitous and tenacious, but they are not universally appealing. Most church members have chosen to associate with larger congregations that provide a full-time, resident pastor, a congregation-owned building, and a variety of programs based on age and interests.

Various mainline denominations differ in the size of their average congregation (from less than one hundred to more than two hundred), but in each, the statistical distribution of members remains roughly the same: 15 percent of the largest churches reach 50 percent of the membership; 50 percent of the smallest churches serve 15 percent of the members.[5] Yet the distribution of clergy serving these two groups is about equally divided: about as many pastors work with the largest 15 percent of churches (with half the denominational membership) as work with the smallest 50 percent of congregations (with less than one-fifth of the denominational membership). In addition to professionally trained and ordained clergy, the larger congregations usually have several employed persons on the church staff, including musicians, educators, secretaries, and maintenance personnel. Based on their resources and organization, larger churches often pride themselves on a "full program, with something for every member of the family."

Further, larger congregations of Anglo-Americans are more frequently located in residential neighborhoods of metropolitan areas, or in growing suburban communities.[6] Their members typically are well-educated, management-oriented, and live in single-family homes. They are the consumers for the program materials and church publications. The church literature that they receive does not ignore the small church. It simply filters "smallness" through concepts and values that are acceptable (or at least understandable) to the market of large church members who buy the literature. Small churches are usually portrayed as miniature versions of the larger congregations. The uniqueness of the small church is ignored or unknown.

In the late twentieth century, the small church was rediscovered by the religious publishers and even the secular media. It is ironic that the oldest, most universal, and largest number of churches needed to be "rediscovered" by the denominational leaders and the press. This rediscovery can be understood in the light of the growth concerns that have dominated the agenda of most denominational organizations. With the pent-up population exploding into new subdivisions following World War II, the church responded with a commitment to expand and a theology of church growth. The Civil Rights Movement ignited a drive for rights for racial groups, people with disabilities, women, and gays and lesbians that challenged the social conscience of the churches. Growth and change became two dominant themes of mainline churches.

As growth and change dominate the church agenda, the small church seems out of sync. Against the denominational mandates to grow, most small churches remained at about the same number of members. In the battles of social conscience principles, most small churches placed a priority on personal relationships. In the dramatic encounters of our times, small churches often did not fit denominational agendas. And they are unlikely to engage in sudden growth, nor are they likely to shake the social order. But they will remain. Small churches will continue to be the quiet majority of Protestant congregations, marching to a different drummer.

History is on the side of the small church. The large church is the new kid on the block. Historically, Protestant denominations in the United States have depended on small churches. At the time of the Civil War, the size of the average Protestant church was less than one hundred members. A few large churches were in the center of the city, or at the center of the ethnic community. By the end of that century, the average congregation still had less than one hundred fifty members.[7] Through the nineteenth century, most of the frontier clergy received at least part of their income from secular employment. The church was primarily a neighborhood experience, locally supported and locally financed.

Two organizational changes early in the twentieth century have affected the small church. First, small churches have seen the rise and decline of denominational structures that organized resources, developed programs, projected strategies, and claimed the allegiance of the participating congregations. Small churches, once nurtured through networks of personal relationships, had to learn how to work with organizational committees and staff. Second, a few congregations that have grown into very large megachurches dominate the media landscape. These large congregations—typically located in the suburbs near an arterial highway—have eclipsed the Old First Church that once was the denominational flagship at the center of the larger cities or towns in the area.

Despite the dominating shadow of megachurches, they represent less than 1 percent of the congregations in the United States. The vast majority of congregations desire a more modest goal— to have a full program of worship, education, and fellowship based on their own financial resources and to be served by at least one professionally trained, full-time pastor as a generalist (not a specialist) who could meet the wide range of congregational needs. But the expanding market for program materials especially tailored for larger congregations emphasized a new need: the specialist, who brought particular skills to a team of paid leaders. Specialist clergy served in denominational staff and larger congregations that had greater financial resources. They set new standards above what the small congregation might provide. The lowest salary on a staff of specialists is invariably higher than the average income for a small church pastor of the same denominational family.

Organizational efficiency, often equated with bigness, dominates the self-image of many church members as well. In some denominations, the primary new employment opportunities occur in specialties for larger congregations such as institutional chaplain, pastoral counselor, and program staff. These positions become pacesetters for professional success, and a standard by which to set new rates for clergy compensation.

In the face of these changes, the small church is not only tenacious and ubiquitous, but also out of step. It does not fit the organizational model for management efficiency. It does not conform to the program expectations of "something for everyone." It does not provide expanding resources for professional compensation. It is not a "success."

Unfortunately, denominational leaders have contact with small churches only when the small churches have problems. Church committees and consultants with experience in larger congregations are asked advice about the maladies of being small. They appear in time of crisis, like medical specialists who have never known the patient. They are experts in such topics as finance and membership growth. They come from larger churches and bring programs that have worked before, in other places. It is a compassionate deed, an act of charity. Sometimes the medicine works. Usually the change is not lasting, and the residue is mutual frustration.

In offering this book to the reader, I run the same risks of analysis, unsuitable recommendations, and mutual frustration. Because I have seen the pragmatism of leadership and the resilience of small-church members, I doubt if these few thoughts will abuse anyone, and I trust they will prove useful to some. I have made assumptions in the development of this material:

First, enough has been said about the limitations and weaknesses of the small church in comparison with larger organizations. I will try to describe the small church in its own integrity and beliefs. I will not knowingly avoid problem areas, but I will try to see them in context, and not in comparison, with other churches.

Second, I will stick as closely as possible to the questions and the insights offered by pastors and people of small congregations, and church leaders who have worked with them over the years. Clearly, I have my personal biases and blindness. I wish that I were more conscious of these limitations, but for that point I must depend upon the good will of the reader and the guidance of the Holy Spirit.

Third, my organization of the material is based on a perspective that I believe is both theologically supported and sociologically evident. I believe that small churches are intrinsically different from larger organizations. They have many of the same concerns: money, buildings, personnel, outreach. But people who choose small churches approach their problems differently. The small church is not an organization; it is an association that generates and lives by its social capital.[8]

Fourth, I have chosen to follow one particular approach to the exclusion of many alternatives. I have tried to let the theological and sociological implications unfold as the book progresses. This approach has the double risk of ignoring important areas for consideration, and overstating certain perspectives on the areas considered. For my oversights on the one hand, and my advocacy on the other, I warn the reader to beware. I recognize that "ideal types" are unreal, and they never exist in practice. At the same time, I have consciously chosen to present a consistent approach, citing many examples, with the hope that those who see and understand this perspective will take the germ of an idea or insight and let it grow very differently from anything that I had conceived or anticipated.

Specifically, the book is divided into three parts: Part 1, *Caring*, will focus on the implications of smallness in the intimacy of membership. We shall consider the implications of "primary relationships" among members who know one another perhaps too well, and have done so for perhaps too long. In such a primary group, we shall consider the prospects for membership growth, church program, and pastoral care.

Part 2, *Belonging*, will explore the interaction in faith and theology among the members of small churches, and between the church and its community. We shall look at the way small churches develop character based on their perspectives of culture, time, and place.

Part 3, *Sharing*, will seek to distinguish the way particular congregations express their character and deal with their problems. We shall take special note of conflict in small churches, different types of congregations and the styles they express, and the interaction between small churches and denominational programs.

Since this material was generated and expanded by countless workshops, each chapter will be introduced by an engagement exercise. Since personal relationships lie at the heart of the small-church experience, the exercises are designed to offer the reader a sense of personal participation and local application.

The praxis that combines faith and practice in small churches should point toward a more important theological affirmation—that small churches embody and enact their faith far better than they explain it. Each of the sections—caring, belonging, and sharing—constitutes a faith statement-in-action by small churches. Like a theological text, the actions of the small church must be "read" as their testimony of faith. Steeped in biblical foundations, small churches are ready to let their living do their talking. This book attempts to listen, and respond.

Suggestions for Further Reading

Ammerman, Nancy T. et al. *Studying Congregations: A New Handbook*. Nashville: Abingdon Press, 1998.
   Basic tools for congregational self-discovery and action in community context.

Coote, Robert B., ed. *Mustard Seed Churches: Ministries in Small Churches*. Minneapolis: Fortress Press, 1990.
   Collected essays on many dimensions from practice to theory, theory to practice.

Putnam, Robert D. *Bowling Alone: The Collapse and Revival of American Community.* New York: Simon and Schuster, 2000.
 Affirmation of "social capital" that puts small churches on the cutting edge.

Taylor, Nick. *Ordinary Miracles: Life in a Small Church.* New York: Simon and Schuster, 1993.
 In this good story, the character and characters of a small church come alive.

PART ONE

Caring

To understand the small church, we begin with the feelings of the members. When asked, members show a strong sense of ownership and deep feelings of belonging. "This is *our church*," they say. Members do not begin with apologies or comparisons, unless they are implied because the questioner comes from a larger congregation. For members, the small church is not "small but beautiful," or "small but quality," or "small but *anything*." Members have a strong, positive attitude toward belonging, because it is a significant experience in their lives. Some "members" are not active in church programs, or regular in attendance, or even registered on church rolls. They may participate only on special occasions and attend only for annual events. Even without official membership, it remains "*our* church" to them. They have remained with the church despite other alluring alternatives. In times of crises for the congregation, they have rallied with support. In the crises of their personal families, the congregation has surrounded them with care and concern. Belonging to the church is like being a member of the family.

Part 1 presents the unique character of small-church *caring*. The discussion is based on the concept of *primary relationships* that provide the strength of belonging in small churches. In chapter 2, I consider the *place of persons* in the group. Chapter 3 raises the problems of *growth*. Chapter 4 considers questions of *program* and *leadership*.

The Choreography of Worship

The place of worship has accumulated meaning for those who attend. The way people enter, sit, participate, and depart is a folk dance in slow motion, a *choreography of worship*. In this exercise, we observe the dance of our own worship.

The exercise is best done if people work separately at first and then share preliminary results. Over a period of weeks, they can test their findings by checking the seating of people throughout the sanctuary, and by talking with particular people about the meaning of their "place."

Procedure

Draw a diagram of the sanctuary, especially noting the location of the pews or chairs, the pulpit, the choir, and other seating arrangements.

Mark the place where you sit. (In your mind, sit there and imagine looking around.) Enter the initials or nicknames to indicate where other people usually sit. Add as many people as possible before you continue the exercise. Finally, put a circle around the initials of those with whom you usually speak before or after worship.

When you have gone as far as you can alone, share your diagram with others who are working on the project. You might also consult a membership list of the congregation. Make a note of the people whom you remembered first, and those whom you could not remember until reminded.

With the faces, the concerns, and the prayers of these people in mind, we are ready to consider the caring qualities of the small congregation.

The Caring Cell

If membership is so satisfying in small churches, then why do they not attract more people? If we know these churches appeal to relatively few people, then why would their members work so hard and give so much of themselves to keep the church open? In a rational, cost-benefit analysis, perhaps it doesn't make sense. The strength and lasting appeal of the small congregation can be best understood through the sociological insights of the "primary group." As seen in the responses from the congregations in the FACT Report, the small-church experience (defined as under 100 Regularly Participating Adults[1]) "feels like a close-knit family." (Fig. 2)

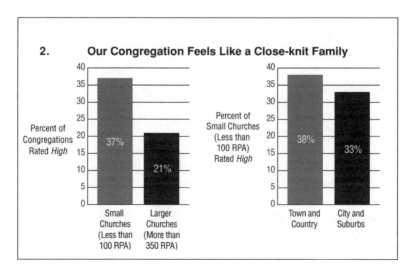

The Primary Group

In a primary group, members enjoy seeing themselves as "family," as suggested in the FACT data above. They feel more united by common interests, beliefs, tasks, and territory. They are not self-conscious about their relationships and are bound together more by sentimental ties than by contractual agreements. They have solidarity, a feeling of belonging, intimacy and personal bond. The primary group is a folk society in the midst of the industrial culture. When so many other contacts are temporary and impersonal, the primary group provides the atmosphere of an extended family. In the widely used definition of Charles Cooley, "[Primary groups] are primary in several senses, but chiefly in that they are fundamental in forming the social nature and ideals of the individual."[2]

Like the primary group, the small church develops and confirms the ideals of individuals in the context of its own character and strength. Like the primary family group, the small church offers intimacy and reassurance among those who can be trusted. Like the extended family, many small churches have a territorial identity with a particular place. Its turf may be the rural crossroads or the urban *barrio* or the old neighborhood or even the developing suburb. Like the family-clan, the church family often carries the food and culture of a particular ethnic, racial, or national group. Faith is transmitted through the cultural artifacts. In this caring group, people who claim a common heritage can share the rhythm of the seasons and the silence of life's transitions. Over time, these relationships are the rich soil that grows "social capital," which Robert Putnam feels has been lost in the fast pace and social mobility of contemporary life.[3]

Personal relationships are the basis of the primary group. At best, such relationships are warm, intimate, spontaneous, and personally satisfying. But not always; primary groups may become hot, cruel, petty, and irrational. Cooley continues, "It is not to be supposed that the unity of the primary group is one of mere harmony and love. It is always a differentiated and usually a competitive unity."[4] Primary groups have a capacity to embrace a variety of motives and enhance a wide range of "characters." People are cared for, even in the tensions of strained relationships. Primary groups may be demanding at critical moments, inhibiting, or even smothering to the creativity of individual members. If their relationships were contractual, members might be free to leave. But they stay, because their roots are far deeper than reason or contract. Members are held by experiences, community caring, and according to Theodore H. Erickson, their "own integrity, shaped by biblical, historical, and cultural roots."[5]

Primary groups typically react to their environment with a "live and let live" attitude. On the one hand, they present a solid front. Although they fight within the family, they will close ranks if approached by an outsider. Oppression increases the commitment of members to one another. Sometimes they cling to imagined oppression as a means of group solidarity.[6] At the same time, they have no need to control the environment in order to prove their identity. Members receive their satisfaction from the time shared, from being together and caring for one another. Additional achievements are almost accidental, not essential to the group.[7] Like the flower in the wall, the beauty of the group together is its own excuse for being.

Primary Groups in Larger Churches

The small group is, of course, the building block of every congregation. Larger churches may have many such small groups to provide for mutual sharing and support. Church groups are organized around prayer, study, and service; around age groups, men's and women's interests; around the concerns of couples, families, single persons, the young, and the elderly; around planning for events, sharing social interests, enjoying recreation, engaging in social causes. In a congregation of five hundred members, about half the membership will feel like they belong to one or more church groups, and a person who belongs to one group will usually participate in several. Many of these groups provide the members with the satisfactions of primary relationships in the context of the larger congregation.

Most of the published program materials are designed to be used in small groups and sub-groups. The materials will have suggestions for ways to organize the church group around various interests, tasks, skills, and objectives to accomplish the stated goals. This pattern is characteristic of women's organization manuals, education materials, fund-raising, membership recruitment, and even development and evaluation of worship. Some of these task committees do become primary groups as members share while they are working together.

Small-group processes have been especially effective in incorporating members in churches located in communities of high mobility. Although the population may experience a rapid turnover, the churches have used highly structured small groups to develop common tasks and to provide a sense of accomplishment in a common product. This can be done in a relatively short cycle, with different start-up times for the groups, resulting in waves of groups that flow through the life of the church. Small groups have become the living cells of a much larger church body. But small churches are not simply smaller versions of the larger church. They are unique. They are not multi-celled organizations with a common base. Small churches are a *single cell* of caring that includes the whole congregation.

The Single Cell of People-in-Place

The small congregation is the appropriate size for only one purpose: the members can know one another personally. Not all the members can know all the others on a continuing, face-to-face basis, but they can all know about one another. They expect to be able to "place" everyone physically and socially in the fabric of the congregation. The caring-cell church may be defined as a primary group in which the members expect to know, or know about, all other members.

In a specifically physical sense, members can associate the name with the face, the face with the family, and the family with the place where each person sits in worship. Those people whom they do not know personally, or who may not be regular in attendance at worship, can be placed through various connections in the congregation and in the community, such as relatives, friends of relatives, neighbors and neighbor's neighbors, place of employment, home residence (perhaps remembered by the name of a former owner[8]), and so on. Everyone has a place that can be located in the fabric of the congregation.

When using the "Choreography of Worship" exercise, I found that most people are uncomfortable when they are asked to say why they sit where they do. Those who answer quickly usually have a functional reason: "I can hear better," "To take up the collection," "It's my seat in the choir," or "I can avoid the draft." All these sound reasonable, until we ask people to move. Then we discover there is an emotional relationship, more than a functional relationship, between the person and the pew.

"She was livid," said the astonished pastor, "and she is not like that. I thought she would hit him with her cane." The pastor was describing an elderly woman who found her pew preempted by a visitor. The woman later apologized and said that she did not know "what possessed me." Our reasons for our choice of pew may sound rational to us, but after a time we become attached to "our place." If people are frustrated in reaching their place, they become quite anxious; if asked to move, they become downright hostile. "The territorial principle motivates all of the human species,"[9] says Robert Ardrey, and we remember the gentle woman with her cane in the air.

Most people cannot say exactly why they sit where they do, or why they would not feel right if they worshiped in another pew. But they usually can remember the names of the people who have shared that pew with them, and who first brought them to that spot. One father said that he used to sit across the church, and his son sat in this pew. But his son went to serve in the army, and he returned in a coffin, so "I like to sit next to where he sat before he left home." One young man said, "This is where we have always sat," but he is new to the congregation and his family is a thousand miles away. In a congregation with a long history, one older woman said that she was unwilling to move because "I might be sitting in someone's pew, although of course they have mostly died. Still, it is their place . . ." One gentleman said he sat where he did simply because "that's always been my seat."

A minority of members does not sit in a consistent location. Some will move around in one of two or three choices. If pressed, they will usually recall the faces of those with whom they have shared those places, and moving is almost like visiting. Others seem to want to "float" to visit with people, and to provide for their own need for personal space.[10] Even without a place, their space has a sense of others, a relationship to the worshiping community.

The pew and the sanctuary as a whole can be seen as "people-space." Through the mixture of faces and experiences, empty space and physical objects begin to take on a sustained significance in our lives.[11] The act of worship becomes a "folk dance" in slow motion, a graceful gliding of people seeing the familiar and touching the friendly as they enter, take their places, renew their sense of the Lord's loving care, and "depart in peace." As one sensitive pastor said of an old, stiff congregation, "Everyone is in the procession, not just the choir!" It is the choreography of worship, as regular and as beautiful as any dance on stage.

When do the members arrive, and what is their pattern of entry? What reason do they offer for their seating, with whom do they visit, and what is their pathway of departure? The choreography of worship may say more about a member's theology than the Scripture they hear and creeds they recited. Further, the "worship-dance," with its fixed positions and locations of the people, may say more of the history and commitments of the congregation than all the printed chronicles.[12]

Absent and Invisible Members

Physical place has a special impact on the sense of well being among the members of the congregation. The presence of people in their places creates a positive climate for congregational activities. The absence of someone has an impact throughout the congregation. When someone is not in his or her place, others *feel* the absence. Thus, the pastor of an urban, ethnic-family congregation notes, "Those who attend worship know everyone else, to whom they are related, and where they work; and they become very anxious when someone misses a worship service." The empty pew in worship has much the same impact as the empty chair at the evening meal of a large family: everything may be all right, but the family feels incomplete.

The member who missed worship is apt to be called, not just to be reminded that someone cares. He or she is reprimanded for being absent, because the absence "hurt" the pattern of seating in worship. Others felt the absence and respond, sometimes in anger.

At the same time, there are other people in worship who may be "invisible." The choreography of worship can be a very disturbing exercise to the pastor, and to the elders, deacons, and vestry when we discover that some people are "invisible"—that is, they are not even remembered as part of the worship experience. This is the typical response of the exercise in a larger congregation: fewer people have fixed seats, and most people only remember their own stratum in the congregation (age, friendships). But in the caring cell of the small church, the officers should be able to place all the regular worshipers. The ones forgotten are often those who most need the care of the congregation: the elderly who sit alone, the young people who seek some independence, and the children who are quietly part of the family (the noisy children and youth are remembered first, with negative feelings). In some congregations, strangers and visitors are clearly evident, but often "invisible" to congregants in a hurry to see their friends. Priority of memory offers insight into the caring style of the congregation.

Seating in the sanctuary is symbolic of the caring cell. Everyone has a place in the fabric of the group. The group is whole (*shalom*, "at peace") when the people are present.

Social Order and Social Place

The experience of belonging to a small congregation meets a basic human need for social order and metaphysical orderliness. Order, says Peter Berger, is "a protective structure of meaning, erected in the face of chaos. Within this order the life of the group as well as the life of the individual makes sense. Deprived of such order, both group and individual are threatened with the most fundamental terror, the terror of chaos that Emil Durkheim called *anomie* (literally, a state of being 'order-less')."[13] In the small congregation, the rhythm of the week begins and ends with everything and every person to be found in his or her rightful place. Berger continues:

> [Humanity's] propensity for order is grounded in a faith or trust that, ultimately, reality is "in order," "all right," "as it

should be." Needless to say, there is no empirical method by which this faith can be tested. To assert it is itself an act of faith. But it is possible to proceed from the faith that is rooted in experience to the act of faith that transcends the empirical sphere. . . . In this fundamental sense, every ordering gesture is a signal of transcendence.[14]

Ordering of events and people can be seen as the backbone, the hard skeleton, for the life of the social body. The pulse of routine events and the placing of particular people provide the framework within which life is predictable and people are nurtured. "At the very center of the process of becoming fully human, at the core of *humanitas,* we find an experience of trust in the order of reality," Berger affirms. Ordering and caring are two sides of the same coin. Once order has been affirmed, Christian caring can embrace a larger community.

Members of small churches "place" people in more than their seats in the sanctuary. The small church is often only the formal gathering of a much larger community, sometimes only the tip of the iceberg. Members have a social place, not just in the church but also in the larger community: they are known by family—the people to whom they are related, or to whom they were related, or sometimes to whom they *ought* to be related. A few members in a relaxed evening can draw relationships (sociometrics) between almost everyone on the parish list, and often even more people who are not on the list.

The small church retains the "village sensitivity" to people, even in the most urban setting. Perhaps especially in the city, the church provides ties to the social turf. Members care for those who have made confession and communion, and for many more. They care for the extended families of church families and "to all that are far away" (Acts 2:39). They care for the whole "village."

Miniature Multi-celled Churches

History and location make a difference, as suggested in the FACT data above. Small town and country churches with more social stability see themselves as closer family than large churches, but also so do small churches in the city and suburbs. Further, not all churches with fewer than two hundred members are single cells of caring Christians whose members expect to know one another personally.[15] For example, old Holy Trinity Church in a changing urban community may have been left behind when the membership moved to the suburbs, and several layers of new residents who took their places in the neighborhood. Typically, such an Old First Church will have a small membership, a large building, and many empty rooms. Often it will continue to print a full roster of church groups, with something for everyone and a leader for every group. But the population has changed, the membership shrunk, and the groups no longer meet. It may be a small church in size of membership, but it remains a multi-celled mindset among its old members, and in its organizational structure. It limps along with unfilled cells. The key difference is in the attitude of the members. They do not expect to know everyone and do not feel the need to place everyone who comes in the door. Carried by cherished memories, they maintain many cells, but simply do not have enough members to fill them. The multi-celled church is typically open and waiting. The single-cell church is less open but more durable. The multi-celled church is designed for diversity and expansion.

The Implications of Social Place

In this chapter, we introduce four implications of the simple caring cell that will be expanded in subsequent chapters. First, the caring cell provides an arena for healing and for caring. Second, the intensity of concern forces some delineation of boundaries between people that sometimes appear as social distance or even hostility. Third, the caring cell provides its own cocoon for time and space. Fourth, social space is difficult to enter. Because these themes are interdependent, we shall introduce them together and then consider them separately.

(1) Beneath the sense of wholeness when people are "in place" lies a concern for the physical health as well as the presence of members. When the absence of a person "hurts," then health is not an idle concern. "How are you?" is a question, not just a social greeting. The one who asks must have time to listen to an answer. For the busy pastor or committee chairperson, no business can be transacted until the question of health has been settled.

Caring has a healing effect upon the one cared for and upon those who initiate the caring. Caring has a way of putting our lives in perspective, our priorities in place. Milton Mayerhoff, in his little book *On Caring,* describes the effect:

> In the context of a [person's] life, caring has a way of ordering his [or her] other values and activities around it. When this ordering is comprehensive, because of the inclusiveness of his [or her] carings, there is a basic stability in his [or her] life; he [or she] is "in place" in the world. . . . My feeling of being in-place is not entirely subjective, and it is not merely a feeling, for it expresses my actual involvements with others in the world. . . . [Place] is not assured once and for all, for it is our response to the need of others to grow which gives us place.[16]

Caring and place are so intimately interdependent that they offer the means that most small churches use to involve their congregations in community caring and Christian witness. These program themes will be examined further in chapter 6.

(2) Social space implies an intimacy that is more than many people want or need. Members of small congregations handle intimacy differently. Some members enjoy the contact, the support, and the flow of information. One pastor complained: "I serve the best community grapevine in the county—but they never produce anything but juicy stories. Why don't they talk about something important?" They do: they talk about people.

Other members react to intimacy with a kind of formality, even toward those who have been well known to them from childhood. For example, one pastor in the Midwest told of being introduced by the clerk of the congregation to one of the leading citizens of the town. Each addressed the other by the title "Mister." Only months later did he discover that they had grown up together, "climbed the same apple trees, and dammed the same streams." Like workmen who are forced to live together in the wilderness, the two old friends had assumed a posture of distance to protect themselves from too much intimacy.

A third way of handling intimacy is through aggression. If too many people are too closely pressed, a certain amount of hostility defines the internal boundaries and clears the air for continued socializing. Some of the conflict has become stylized and socially tolerable, but some is personally and socially destructive. We shall consider these questions in chapter 8.

(3) Social space provides a cocoon in which significant experiences can be remembered and replayed. In congregations where personal relationships are primary, there develops a stabilizing sense of timing, noticeable in the rhythm of the worship hymns and the cyclical events of the changing seasons. This community measures time in terms of significant experiences, and space in terms of the people who share it. This is a relational theology where God makes himself known in people-places, and people-times.

A theology of relationships affirms the past: family, important people, significant events, and "historic" places. The fabric of memory anticipates perpetuity. Perhaps the individual will be gone, but the congregation will remain. In this context, mere temporal problems seem insignificant. When confronted with a budget that could not be balanced, the church treasurer simply nodded, saying, "Yes, hmm." There was no solution immediately available, no suggestion for dealing with the problem, no expectation that a resolution would be found soon, if ever. Neither was there any hint of resignation or thought of closing. The theological implications of social place will be considered in Part 2.

(4) Social space is hard to enter. When the members are asked why they belong, they usually do not single out the pastor or the program. More often they remember a time when they were in need and the church "carried us through the crisis." When we draw the lines of care between members, we often have an image of a many-pointed star. When we try to lay hold of the caring cell, it often feels like a "prickly ball" of Christian love. The members' experiences have bound them together, but also separated them from the rest of the world. Like all primary groups, the caring cell is hard to enter.

One pastor and his wife visited a Reformed congregation with roots in Eastern Europe and were warmly received before the worship. They looked forward to the communion, since the elements were homemade bread and wine. But when the worship began, "everything was conducted in the native language, the prayers, the hymns, everything. It seemed like we were intruders. . . . Even the youth are beginning to stay away."

Entry into such congregations, even where everyone speaks a common language, might seem like eating a loaf of heavy peasant bread—that is, its inner texture promises to be sweet and delicious if we manage to break through the solid crust. This experience of inner texture and outer toughness is universal in primary groups. But, as everyone with in-laws knows, it may take a long time to become one of the family. Those inside are usually satisfied, but what of the others? The problem of new members will be the subject of the next chapter.

Summary of a Caring Cell

Many small churches can be described as caring cells because of the primary relationships of their members. I do not presume that the caring cell will explain every variety of small church, or fit every dimension of church life. For some congregations it may not fit at all.[17] But I believe that this description offers a constructive approach for seeing the small church with its strengths and limitations. This approach offers certain immediate implications:

- Human relationships are primary. These relationships may become attached to events and to objects in a much more specific way than in other, larger congregations that have diversity of interests and rapid turnover of membership.
- Human relationships form a caring cell in which everyone has a place. Since the absence of a member hurts the sense of belonging, the energies of the congregation can more easily be directed to concerns of physical and mental health. Small congregations are especially sensitive to hospital calling, prayers for healing, and the power of God to make people whole.
- The rhythm of the right people in the right place satisfies a human need for order in the ministry of the small church. Orderliness is the skeleton of the caring, Christian congregation. At times, the urge for order and routine seems to dominate over the will to care for people.
- Churches develop character from their unique experiences. When that character is identified, the congrega-

tion may be motivated more from a sense of Christian "pride" than from a desire for new accomplishments.

- Since people are most important, the caring cell can be aroused to help particular people in need. "When the need is clear, the response is overwhelming," said one appreciative executive.

- Finally, many people find a peculiar strength and serenity when they are seated in their place. Pastors who are willing to sit in the pew *with* their people often discover an otherwise unknown array of burdens and an untapped source of spiritual strength. One pastor sat for several minutes in silence with an elderly woman of his congregation. Then he recorded her prayer:

Lord, I'm tired—so very tired. Please, Lord, I don't want any advice. I've heard enough of that over the years. I don't want to be told what I must do. I've been told that often enough. Lord, I just want to sit here in quietness and feel your presence. I want to touch you and to know your touch of refreshment and reassurance. Thank you for this sacred little spot where I have heard your voice and felt your healing touch across the years. Thank you for these dear friends who share this pew with me. Together we have walked the tear-lined lanes. We know what it is to be lonely. . . . We also know comfort and strength of one another and the joy of your presence. O God, the child of my womb has become a drunk. . . . Daily I watch her die before my eyes. Where have I failed, O Lord? How can I find the strength to continue? How can I help my dying daughter find herself?

O God, soon I will be going home to be with you and my husband. I am ready, even eager. But until that day help me to be a help to others. Give me strength to live this day and peace to enjoy it. Amen.

He called his experience, including the silence, "listening to the pew speak."

Suggestions for Further Reading

Anthony G. Pappas, ed. *Five Small Stones: A Newsletter for Small Churches*. Providence, R.I.
   The most constant, current information source for small-church leaders.

Frank, Thomas Edward. *The Soul of the Congregation: An Invitation to Congregational Reflection*. Nashville: Abingdon Press, 2000.
   Place and time, narrative and organization—a rhythm of analysis and action.

Pappas, Anthony G., *Entering the World of the Small Church*. Bethesda, Md.: Alban Institute, 2000.
   A practitioner who has immeasurably enriched the leadership of small churches.

Ray, David R. *The Indispensible Guide to Smaller Churches*. Cleveland: Pilgrim Press, 2002.
   Encyclopedia-like overview of small-church issues and concerns.

CHAPTER THREE EXERCISE

Gatekeepers, Patriarchs, and Matriarchs

In small congregations, several functions are particularly important in helping new members become part of the congregation. Several people may perform these functions, and sometimes different people take turns. One function is the gatekeeper,[1] and another is the patriarch or the matriarch. Using the seating sketch from the "Choreography of Worship" exercise, circle the gatekeeper(s) in green, and star the patriarch(s) and matriarch(s) in yellow. They may be identified as follows:

The *gatekeepers* linger around the edge of the church meetings and congregational worship. They are often older, often male. Although they usually do not have positions of leadership, they enjoy greeting everyone, especially visitors. They like to know everyone and everything, but they avoid being at the center of events. One pastor reports that "during the sermon they go outside, just to talk." They may not agree with what the church is doing, but they enjoy explaining it to others. Gatekeepers will be found near the "gates" of the group. More likely, they will find you.

The *patriarchs and matriarchs* are at the center of the church. They sit in the center of the sanctuary, and they feel in the center of the congregation. They may have wealth and be involved in many activities, or they may have passed their prime. They may be friendly, or aloof. One pastor describes a matriarch as "gruff on the outside, but a very caring person." They may no longer sit on the official boards of the church. But they have one essential feature: patriarchs and matriarchs have lived through the historical moments of the church. In their presence, they carry the identity of the church. They remember when things were different, and "how we got to where we are."

CHAPTER THREE
Growth by Adoption

How can a small church grow? This puzzle lies at the heart of the small-church enigma. There are four answers to this question. They are in apparent contradiction. Yet, like an ancient riddle, most small churches could give the same four answers, despite apparent contradictions:

Our small church has grown.
Our small church can't grow.
Our small church could give up its smallness and become a larger congregation.
Our small church can absorb new "members" by using its natural gifts more creatively.

Our Small Church Has Grown

Most small churches have already grown much bigger than they "ought to be." They look small only when compared with the larger organizational churches that flourish in metropolitan communities. If we define church by the "business B's" of religious institutions—budgets, buildings, and bodies—the small church comes on the short end. But the small church appears much stronger when measured by human relationships. If the church is defined by the number of people who know (or want to know) about one another personally, then the small church has grown.

The genius of the small church is that everyone knows, or knows about, everyone else. In the small church, everyone has a place. Everyone has a place to sit and a place in the social fabric of the congregation. In larger congregations, the subgroups are considerably smaller than the whole congregation of a small church. For example, one fellowship group may have thirty or forty members; a committee or a study group may have fifteen or twenty participants; a prayer cell or a sharing group may not tolerate more than eight or ten people. In larger congregations, members may know persons in one or more other groups.

The small church is a single cell of caring Christians. The membership may be only one hundred people, or even fewer. But the network of people who care for one another may be much greater. A better measure of church size might be the number of people who are included in the ministry, who turn to the pastor in time of need, or who support the church at Christmas, Easter, and the annual pancake festival. If the church has a long association with a piece of land and a particular cultural heritage, it may still have the mentality of a small church and yet embrace two hundred, perhaps three hundred or more people who meet the criteria. They know each other personally, by family, name, and place in the community, as we see frequently in congregations that are united by language, tradition, and the smell of familiar cooking.

The small church has grown. If measured by the impact of the church upon the relationships of its members, many small churches are already much larger than their more "successful" suburban sisters. Churches with larger memberships are typically collections of several smaller groups. In small churches, more people know more people, and know more about more people, than in most larger congregations. In the relationships among people, the small, single-cell church is much larger than any one cell in the larger congregations. When compared to other kinds of caring groups, the small church is much larger than it is perceived to be. When church size is measured by human relationships, the small church may be the largest expression of the Christian faith.

Our Small Church Can't Grow

The small church can't grow, but not for the reasons that the church itself usually advances, and not for the limitations often whispered by denominational committees. Church members usually claim that they would like for their churches to grow. Most church leaders say they would willingly give up some of their many hats of leadership. At times, they note the lack of growth potential in the community. More often, they are simply baffled by the absence of new members, when the church seems so satisfying to the members who already belong.

Outsiders, and some insiders, whisper uncomplimentary reasons why they believe that small churches can't grow. They say that they are lazy, and small in vision. They note the lack of a "full church program," and urge the addition of particular activities to attract new members. Sometimes they identify the problem with a style of leadership, or the motives of particular people: the officers are afraid of losing their position, or the congregation is "allergic" to new faces.

In their classic study, *Small Town in Mass Society,* Arthur J. Vidich and Joseph Bensman point out the limited prospects for membership growth in a relatively stable community.[2] They designate two sorts of adults who are not church members (the majority of the community): the first are the people who look like good prospects, but don't respond, and the others are people whose lifestyle does not attract the invitation to join. In short, they are the intransigents and the untouchables, which is not a very promising choice.

But the basic obstacle to growth lies in the satisfactions of the present church membership. When the church is seen as one caring cell, the problem is neither complex nor judgmental. The small church is already the right size for everyone to know, or know about, everyone else.[3] This intimacy is not an accident. The essential character of the small church is this capacity to care about people personally. The small church cannot grow in membership size without giving up its most precious appeal, its intimacy.

Small-church members unconsciously feel that they cannot absorb new members without changing the fabric of the group. According to the experts in group dynamics, the small church is already much larger than similar kinds of caring groups.[4] Members often feel the strain. They feel that they cannot receive new members without losing touch with those whom they already know. They cannot make a radical change in the size of the church without losing their motivation for belonging. In the number of people whom they can embrace in Christian care, the members feel, often unconsciously, that they have reached their limit. They cannot grow because, in a word, they feel "stuffed."

"In many cases, the church itself knows that to be small is better," said a pastor in New England. "The members effectively counteract anything the pastor can do to *make* them grow." They may call in the community, or open the building for service to the neighborhood. But most of the members were initially invited by a friend, a relative, or someone they know on their job. Replacements are received almost naturally, but church *growth* is almost impossible.

The church treasurer spoke to the council: "Yes, money is a problem. If we only had a few more members, we could pay the bills." But growth is more than a problem of managing the numbers. For the sake of the budget, they want more members to share the costs. For the salary of the pastor, they could utilize more steady income. But growth in membership affects their satisfactions in belonging. They have reached the limits of their personal compassion. Small-church members are unwilling to change the nature of personal caring for the goal of financial solvency. The small church can't grow while it remains "our small church."

In Christ, members of small churches can love and show concern for all the earth and every living creature on it. But in personal, face-to-face Christian caring, they have drawn the line. They want to "place" everyone who belongs to "our" church. For the sake of knowing and caring, they have set the limit. Their style is not more or less "Christian." It is a choice they have made, and not always consciously.

When an energetic young pastor brought the first five new members into an ethnic congregation of two hundred members, one of the old family members confided, "With so many new faces, I hardly know anyone anymore." She was not unwilling to welcome them. But she knew that "our church" was no longer what it used to be. The small church cannot grow and still remain a small church; it will never be the same. One sensitive urban pastor suggested that the maximum number of new families that the congregation could absorb "could never be more than six or seven each year."

Our Small Church Can Change into a Larger Congregation

Rapid membership growth is possible for many small churches. A substantial minority of small churches could double their membership in the next few years. Rapid membership growth depends less on community potential, more on the values and attitudes of church members. Members of the congregation must want to grow so much that they are willing to give up the satisfactions of knowing, or knowing about, everyone else in the congregation. They must sacrifice the satisfactions of being a small church.

One ironic twist in this phenomenon of smallness emerged from our review of projects in new church development (NCD). In NCD strategy, the mission pastor developed several cell groups of prospective members in homes throughout the community. When a sufficient number of cell groups were organized, the mission pastor tried to unite them to organize a congregation and construct a church building. Some mission pastors were exceptionally gifted in integrating the different cells that had been meeting separately. Other pastors found this process very difficult. The first group of pastors reported their feelings of success in helping the many cells gel into "one big happy family of the church." The second group of pastors worried about their "failure to work out internal differences between the various cell groups." The irony only emerged later when we discovered that the congregations that jelled quickly (thus, "successfully") frequently stopped growing. The other congregations, which seemed to be struggling with their separate, distinctly different cells, continued to increase in membership. They have paid off the first mortgage, sometimes two or three more building mortgages, and are now thriving, "successful" suburban congregations. They have excellent programs, with something for everyone.

The difference is very clear. Members of larger, multi-celled churches cannot know each person in the congregation. They do not expect to know everyone. Larger churches attract and assimilate members through several small units that are "hungry" for members to share a common task. New members do not join the whole church, but become attached to their group. When a group attracts so many members that it becomes unwieldy, the group subdivides to provide space for more new members. Like cells of the human body, the church body has grown by division of large cells into two or more smaller cells.

Most membership growth programs have been designed for large congregations with different groups and diverse interests. These programs have been particularly effective in suburban communities where the population is management oriented and highly mobile. Congregations have taken great pride in what they called a "full church program," from preschool care to programs for the elderly. This program demands a vast variety of social cells, each receptive to new members to fill the necessary functions. The more cells, the more members: the congregation grows by dividing.

Dividing is one activity that the single-cell church refuses to do. A church program with something for everyone is unnecessary when everyone shares emotionally in whatever happens. Members are either present or are immediately informed by the grapevine. Additional church activities are either exhausting or divisive. Growth by division is subversive to the essential satisfactions of belonging to the whole church.

The imperative to grow numerically has been stated most forcefully by the advocates of the Church Growth Movement. C. Peter Wagner writes: "I wish to disassociate myself from the big-church-small-church debate. . . . The optimum size of each church depends primarily on its philosophy of ministry. Churches, much like people, have personalities that set them apart from another." That sounds affirmative, but Wagner continues: "But whether a church is large or it should be a growing church. . . . Healthy large churches and healthy small churches are evangelistically effective." He goes on to note the implications: "If smaller churches are growing they eventually will become large churches. Just as every river was once a stream, every large church was once a small church. When this happens, new small churches will continually be needed."[5]

Wagner describes the growing church, with many different opportunities for participation. Everyone shares in the large celebration, where some anonymity is assumed. Wagner recommends smaller groups within the congregation as a "fellowship circle" of about two hundred worshipers. At the most intimate level, Wagner offers the Christian cell, which "is so close to a family situation that I like to call it a 'kinship circle' to contrast it from the membership circle and the fellowship circle."[6]

That's the logic of church growth, and it works. But the small church must be "converted" to believe that the change is worth the cost. One pastor at a conference on methods of evangelism observed that "any of these methods, if used conscientiously, would turn the small church into a large church, and that's the one thing most small congregations don't want to see happen." Members of the small church know the alternatives, and have made their choice.

Members who joined large and small churches were compared and interviewed in a careful study by Allan Wicker and Anne Mehler.[7] Both groups of new members agreed that large churches have better church schools, more formal worship, more efficient committee organization, and so forth. But they also both agreed that in the small congregation, the members spend more time at church, work harder, know the pastor better, and attend church more regularly. Each group separately seemed more satisfied with the choice that they had made in the church that they had joined than with the alternative.

In a small church, membership growth means a loss of contact with the whole body of the congregation. The members must give up knowing everyone, for the sake of sharing with many more people whom they can never know. Even when members have agreed to try to get their church to grow, they often find that the heart resists.

Pastors who encourage the small church to break into several separate activity groups have received a variety of irrational responses. Some pastors report that members "agree with the programs," but become irritated over petty things "that never bothered anyone before." When one pastor encouraged a series of home meetings to help new members become acquainted, he was accused of "breaking up the church into pieces." In a literal way, he was, and the church grew in membership as a result. When another pastor suggested the need for two, somewhat different Sunday worship services, he was warned that it would "divide the congregation." It did just that: the tension diminished, and each service group prospered for a time.[8] When the community has growth potential, any congregation can grow if the members are willing to let go of their satisfactions in being close to one another. Some small churches are "converted" to larger congregations, with a full program and something for everyone. But they are not small churches anymore.

In the FACT data, we found that small churches are no less willing to incorporate new members, but they are far more likely to be composed of members who have been there all their lives. (Fig. 3a) They simply assimilate new members differently.

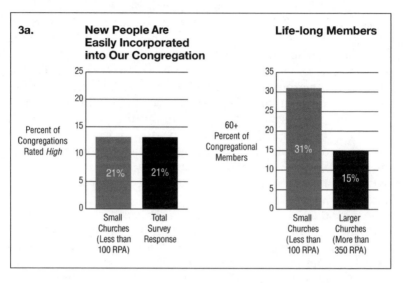

New Members by Adoption

Although small churches may work as hard at incorporating new members, as suggested by the data from FACT above, typically, they must try to absorb new members into the intimate fabric of the congregation. Even in situations where there appears to be no significant membership potential in the community, small churches can bring a few local "intransigents" (as described by one pastor) into the church family. In communities where other churches are rapidly expanding their membership, some congregations steadfastly feel called to remain relatively small as a single-cell congregation. Their new members must be absorbed without pain to resisting members.

The small, caring, single-cell church has many similarities to an extended family. Each offers various levels of participation, and a latitude for individual characters. Members contribute to the whole, yet have a life apart from it. The most natural form of growth for a small church is the way a family grows, by birth and by adoption. Unfortunately, young people who have been born into the small church often leave the community when they become young adults. Some young people will return; many will not.

Adoption is the other way for families to grow naturally. Adoption is a biblical metaphor to describe the way the outsider becomes part of the family of God. According to the Apostle Paul, in his epistles to the Romans (chapter 8) and to the Galatians (chapter 4), we are adopted into God's family through the witness of the Holy Spirit. We were not family, but now we are. The metaphor has already been absorbed into Pauline theology when it is mentioned only in passing in the letter to the Ephesians (chapter 1). Although Paul is most explicit, the process of adoption by God also is implied in the Synoptic Gospels, in John, Hebrews, and Revelation. Even without this specific biblical background, small churches practice growth by adoption.

By adoption, the newcomer joins the history of the family. However, he or she cannot make a unilateral decision to join. Newcomers cannot work their way into the family, to achieve belonging. In the same way, membership in the small church is a shared experience, based on a common faith and mutual understandings. The faith statement of the new member must be mingled with the story or history of the congregation. The adopted member of the church must learn to appreciate the artifacts and traditions of the family, the annual feasts and perennial threats, and the "family secrets" of their history. It takes time to adopt a child. The whole church family must participate.

The adopted member looks in the opposite direction from those who join the small task group of a larger congregation. When new members join a large-church activity, they accept a common goal that holds that group together. In such activity groups, the new member often shares in defining and creating the common future. But adoption looks in the other direction, not to the future, but to the past. The new member is adopted into the family history. The adoptee must absorb the values of the church, just as the church absorbs the new member.

Adoption is less about what you say, and more about who you are. In various forms, adoption includes the faith statements about the Lordship of Christ and discipleship of the believer. But these faith statements must be shared where new members and church leaders share their vulnerability, tell their separate journeys, and emotionally weave together their mutual dependency on one God who cares for all. Participation of church characters, like patriarchs, matriarchs, and gatekeepers, make adoption happen more easily.

Kindred Spirits: Adopting Boomers and Xers

Small churches face a special challenge to reach the next generations—baby boomers (born 1945–1965) and Generation X (born 1966–1985). In many significant ways, the cultural barriers would appear to make the task seem hopeless. Typically, as seen in the FACT data, the membership of smaller congregations is significantly older than large churches, and numerically dominated by a higher percentage of women in the congregation. (Fig. 3b)

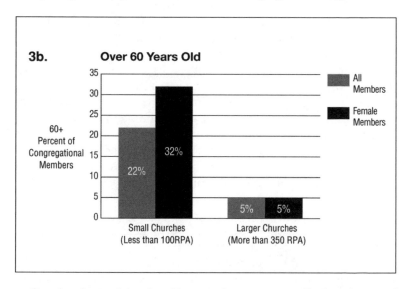

On the face of it, the distance between small churches and young Christians would seem insurmountable. If the caring single cell is difficult to enter for cohorts in the same generation, how much greater is the generation gap from predominately older women to the lifestyles of young families, and even more distance to reach young singles. Consider the clash of traditional continuity that sustains the older group against the constant new discoveries that fed a younger psyche. How might we bridge the differences between veneration for spaces and places that anchors the spiritual life of the older generation with the high mobility and journey theology[9] associated with younger seekers?[10] Music alone would be enough to defeat the enterprise—how can we imagine a worship event that would satisfy everyone from their own comfortable classics to the dissonance of another generation? We have no problem listing the barriers, but bridges would appear more difficult.

- Some small churches have made connections by building on their natural strengths. *Authentic acceptance* is a quality that appeals across generational differences, and can appear in any size congregation.[11] Small churches, where members' concern for each other makes anonymity impossible, affirm and enjoy the uniqueness of every person. Although family values are publicly endorsed, members know too much about each other, and they remember too much about the past, to believe in a cookie-cutter morality for anyone, including, but not limited to, new and younger members. In small congregations, everyone knows the variety of lifestyles that exist in their community, and can tell stories that make more recent diversity seem pale by dramatic comparison. They have always known about dysfunctional families and single parent homes—even before the labels were attached. With encouragement and modeling from leaders, small churches can embrace diversity as long as the person can be located in the social and local network of congregational connections. When confronted with personal contact, they are more likely to relate to the individual person than to catalogue others by race, nationality, marital status, or sexual orientation.
- In addition, small churches have a *faith-style that is compatible with a younger generation.* Historically, members of small churches have preferred to live out their faith rather than depend on theological rationale. They are more likely to embody their beliefs than explain them, and to respond to leaders who model more than preach

about their commitments. The faith-practices that have been identified by Dorothy Bass and her associates are foundational to the life and ministry of small churches, as if these congregations had provided the initial source.[12] Anyone familiar with small churches will recognize the intuitive importance of hospitality, household care, keeping the Sabbath, saying yes and saying no, telling stories (testimonies), healing, dying well, singing and others. Small congregations have built a large network of constituent members who share in the practices of faith, even when they do not officially belong.

- Further, small congregations share with boomers and Xers *respect for primary sources, for example, the Bible and the earth.* They find common ground when congregations create events that celebrate the earth or develop community land for common purposes.[13] Many will come to churches for counseling in transitional moments, and they are responsive in supporting educational and experiential events that explore biblical and cultural foundations, as long as they do not feel trapped into institutional membership.[14] These and other values are shared across generational differences, but not for the younger generation if the price is the loss of personal autonomy.

- Some small churches have taken the bold step to create new categories of relationship to embrace boomers and Xers into their congregational family without branding them with the distasteful label of "church membership." These churches have found a middle ground that has been called "Affiliate Members," "Active Participants," or, my personal choice, "Kindred Spirits." One congregation, after a year of congregational study and conversation, changed the pew cards to add a new response—to the choices of "Member," and "Visitor" they added "Kindred Spirit." The church board defined Kindred Spirit as a participant who shared the ministry but did not become an official member. These Kindred Spirits were added to the parish book and participated in every way as other

members, except they could not vote in official meetings or take a seat on the ruling board of the church.

Kindred Spirits were organizationally unincorporated, but
functionally very active. Indeed, one pastor reported that they
were financially and physically more supportive of the congregation than the typical member, and he threatened "to dissolve the
church rolls and make everyone join all over again." In another
setting, in the month after the church created a recognized place
for Kindred Spirits, thirty members resigned their official status
and signed up as Kindred Spirits.

Gatekeepers, Patriarchs, and Matriarchs

In the exercise at the beginning of this chapter, gatekeepers,
patriarchs, and matriarchs may have seemed irrelevant to the
work of the church. Gatekeepers are often seen as busybodies
because they want to know everything but take so little initiative
in personal leadership. Matriarchs and patriarchs are often difficult to work with, especially in the introduction of new programs.
To the young pastor, they may seem irascible antiquarians.

But in the process of adoption—especially across racial, cultural, and generational differences—the functions of gatekeepers,
patriarchs, and matriarchs are essential. Gatekeepers are the
matchmakers at the door, or the watchful eye from the choir loft.
They may not embody the values of the church or carry the
weight of leadership. But they are gifted with the pleasure of
communication—gab. They like to talk to anyone, especially to
visitors. The gatekeepers interpret the church to prospective
members, sometimes with a glad hand; but at other times they
lock the doors. If the gatekeepers like the match of church and
visitor, adoption is possible.

Matriarchs and patriarchs provide the parent models, the informal officers who recognize and usher the new members into the
family. They complete the process of adoption by sharing the
church history with the new members. New members know they
are accepted when they have heard the stories from the elders
of the church family. New members do not really belong until
they have appreciated the stories and accepted the "old folks"

who shared them. When that time comes, the family covenant is completed.[15]

Gatekeepers, matriarchs, and patriarchs are not the only personalities who keep the small church lively. The reader may wish to look again at the "Choreography of Worship" diagram to identify a wide variety of characters who play a role in the rhythm of life in small churches. In a larger congregation, the Sunday celebration may be more private and reflective. But in the small church, everyone has a part to play. In most small churches, there is the storyteller, the living historian who may embellish for the pleasure of the listeners (who usually have heard it all before). Another common figure is the *first sergeant of the Lord.* He or she makes it clear that he or she is not really in charge, but the one who is in charge is "not immediately available." In the interim, the *sergeant* makes decisions "according to policy." "Mr. Executive Order," he was nicknamed in one congregation. The small church has a way of enhancing and enjoying its characters. Readers might identify other characters, such as the Early Bird, the Scorekeeper, the Sparkplug, the Peacemaker, the Bellringer, and others. Small churches have a way of producing characters, perhaps because they are more visible.

Reservations and Possibilities

Most congregations cannot adopt members until they take pride in their own congregation's story of Christian witness. Much of the friction between old and new members revolves around the private ways in which that history is remembered and the in-group process by which it is shared. Some congregations have facilitated the adoption of new members by asking the oldest (and most liberated) members of the congregation to recall and share—as the oldest person answers the questions of the youngest child in the Jewish Passover. A communicants' class in the evening with church officers, storytellers and matriarchs, surrounded by food, photo slides, family albums, and other artifacts, can bring out much of the informal history of the church.

Adoption should be a part of church growth, but not the alternative or substitute for other appropriate programs. The purpose of "adoption" is to help the pride in a congregation's Christian record become the common property of the congregation, not the private possession of a few. The process of adoption can be just as important for integrating new leadership into the official boards of the church, or even for the entry of a pastor into the life of the congregation.

Adoption is a larger challenge in many congregations where new members are kept on the fringes for several years, or even longer. We should not cheapen the meaning of belonging by trying to rush it, nor should we use adoption as a mask for unchristian snobbishness. This is a question of timing, and motivation. Some of the stories have an intimacy that needs to be cherished. When that intimacy becomes an excuse for exclusion, we have a need to confront one another honestly, in love.[16]

Adoption can bring new life to struggling churches. One inner-city congregation found itself with a handful of elderly members in a culturally changing community. They determined that their ministry was terminal and that the time had come to "retire the church." Since most members had reached the age of retirement, they decided that the church retirement should be fun, that they should do those little things they had always wanted to do together but had been too busy for when they were younger. The church gave up their regular Sunday worship and replaced it with "Fun Time" on Tuesday afternoons. They sang old hymns and prayed together; they read the Bible and had a time of sharing. Sharing time spilled over into a potpourri of quilting, quiet games, old records, a little cooking, and whatever they wanted. They dragged all kinds of old stuff from the closets and cluttered up the social hall with memorabilia. To their surprise, the "Fun Time" was discovered by others living in the neighborhood. Older couples and elderly people living alone began drifting in on Tuesday, though they would never have come on Sunday. The church became crowded and expanded the program. In their retirement, they discovered a booming ministry, which, in time, included its own form of worship and fellowship. When they tried to live out the past, they discovered a new future.

For boomers and Xers, adoption as Kindred Spirits provides a form of "grandparenting," the rediscovery of three generations in families that are far too separated to know more than two generations. Most churches have some semblance of three generations, but usually not in the same families. When new members join by adoption, there comes that happy discovery that the past is important and that the future generation does care—for the person, if not for details of the distant past. A pastor reported such an event when his new-member class joined the officers for a retreat prior to confirmation. One fragment of the conversation ran as follows. Youth: "What was the church like when you joined?" Elderly church officer, thoughtfully: "Just the same." Silence. Youth: "Has the world changed since then?"

Then came the stories of the first time the old man saw an automobile, that "infernal combustion engine," and his own youthful aspiration to be an ostrich farmer. . . . It went for the whole weekend. And it continues several years later. The pastor noted that "grandparenting has a way of happening." Adoption happens when caring reigns.

Suggestions for Further Reading

Caroll, Jackson W. and Wade Clark Roof. *Bridging Divided Worlds: Generational Cultures in Congregations*. San Francisco: Jossey-Bass, 2002.

Comprehensive discussion of real churches reaching younger generations.

Bass, Dorothy C., ed. *Practicing Our Faith: A Way of Life for Searching People*. San Francisco: Jossey-Bass, 1997.

Theology as lived in the simple practices of ordinary lives.

Schaller, Lyle E. *The Small Membership Church: Scenarios for Tomorrow*. Nashville: Abingdon Press, 1994.

A tough challenge for small churches, with practical alternative approaches.

Surrey, Peter J. *The Small Town Church*. Nashville: Abingdon Press, 1981.

Issues for all small churches, but clearly rooted in small towns.

The Pastor's Study and Professional Feelings

The pastor's study is an expression of his or her professional self. In small congregations, the study might be slightly less accessible to members. The study is more likely to be a room in the manse, or in a yoked parish, it may be located in only one of the churches. The maintenance of this space provides important clues about the pastor's self-perception, and the functional fit between pastor and people.

The Pastor's Study

Describe the fixed items essential for work, such as the desk, chairs, lamp, files, bookshelves, computer, phone, fax, and so on. Describe all the intentional decorations, including plants, aquarium, wall hangings, curtains, pictures, diplomas, personal items, and the like. Now describe accidental items of frequent use, such as books, magazines, papers, and program materials. Note which items are professionally significant, and which are personally meaningful. Note where the pastor sits while alone, and while others are present. What might you guess about the values, commitments, and work style of the person who inhabits this office?

Professional Feelings

List at least three satisfactions and at least three frustrations that the pastor feels in his or her ministry and in life with this congregation. If you are a pastor, list for yourself. If you are a church member, list the way you think your pastor feels, and compare your impressions.

CHAPTER FOUR

Pastor/People Tensions

If small churches are such caring cells, then why is there so much tension between pastor and people? As one family said of the old family leadership, "There's a lot of management in our small congregation, and most of it seems to be aimed at keeping the pastor under control." One sweet, caring deacon asked me to help her understand "why our pastor always seems to be in a hurry." One pastor's wife said, "There is a lot of caring in our church, especially for us. But sometimes too much caring will kill you."

Human relationships are the stuff that hold the small caring cell together. Like a good marriage, sometimes these relationships are deeply satisfying, with time to experience them together—but not always, or for everyone. Not all members can tolerate closeness for long periods of time (sometimes for years, or decades, or generations). Sometimes small churches, like big ones, get sick. Sometimes the intimacy of knowing everyone sours into pettiness, nastiness, and abiding mutual dislike. In larger congregations, people can avoid one another and still participate in the life of the church. In small congregations, they are still part of the caring cell, even if they stay home. Even in the most acid relationships, human contact is not broken. "We do not forget to dislike them," is the attitude that many members express.[1]

Pastors use a variety of methods to deal with the intimacy of the caring cell. In a larger congregation, the pastor may deal with members in a more professional role: church meetings, social events, hospital calls, and possibly, scheduled home visits. In a small church, a pastor typically has more frequent contact with more dimensions of the members' lives. At the same time, the members and the whole community may know more about the pastor and his or her family life, even in the city. This personal exposure of the professional minister is basic to pastor/people tensions. In the order of frequency, pastors report their sources of tension revolve primarily around three themes: finance, program development, and the professional self-image of the pastor.[2]

Finances

Money is a sensitive issue in most small congregations.[3] They are always in need, often just surviving. In later chapters, we consider ways of expanding congregational resources. Here we note that financial problems affect the pastor/people relationship directly and continually.

Because the church's income is relatively low, clergy compensation is often the most that the church can offer, and the least that the pastor can live on. As a result, small-church clergy tend to be younger or older than the average pastor, and in some denominations they are more likely to be women. For many young pastors, the small church is viewed as a stepping stone. Some congregations even pride themselves on "the young clergy we have groomed." They are important people, but they do not stay very long.

Clergy provide leadership for the congregation, but usually they do not become part of the community in the same way as those who expect to remain. "Neither his [or her] congregation nor the community regards him [or her] as a permanent resident," report Vidich and Bensman. "Though the minister lives and acts within the community, his [or her] stable referent group lies elsewhere."[4] The clergyperson is often born elsewhere, has a uniquely different education, depends on regional denominational leadership for recognition and advancement, and personally maintains a system of values not completely in harmony with those of the congregation. One pastor said his worst frustration was the "pastor-member gap in seeing the church and the world. . . . The members are frustrated, and so am I." As perceptions differ and frustrations mount, pastors are increasingly apt to seek friendship and support outside of the caring cell of congregational activities.

In the face of all these differences, many pastors are still warmly welcomed by the members of the small church. But the cycle of pastors coming and going leaves a residue of ambivalent feelings. If the pastor's first sermon is too good, the members begin to fear that he or she will not stay very long. If the pastor has the empathy to become part of the caring cell, the members will barter in gifts what they cannot pay in money. The pastor's family will be "treated special." But the final irony is this: if the pastor stays longer than the congregation anticipated, then some members begin to wonder if they have "overestimated our pastor." There grows a shadow of doubt about the pastor's real competence, which can only be dispelled with the rumor that, in fact, the pastor has "turned down several offers in order to stay with us."

On the other side, the pastor personally has another kind of ambivalence about money. Most pastors have unresolved feelings about their compensation: On the one hand, it costs money to live; and on the other hand, they have received a Christian calling. Many small-church pastors have a need for significant salary increases. Yet they feel ambivalent about raising the subject directly with the officers or the congregation. For many pastors the rift is not between pastor and people, but the source of the conflict is within the pastor—between the desire to serve the Lord and the need for a modest income.

Two powerful figures appear important in this drama: the pastor's spouse (especially the wife) and the church treasurer. The wives of small-church pastors are not more frequently employed than the wives of other pastors, but the motivation is different: wives of small-church pastors are more often employed because of insufficient income to meet family expenses.[5] Further, because of their own professional training, the wives of rural pastors often feel that there is no appropriate place of employment that matches their qualifications. In an urban or rural setting, if the spouse has satisfactory employment, the pastor is more likely to extend his or her stay in the community. In my experience, the spouse's job satisfaction appears to be more important than the pastor's evaluation of his or her church ministry. This marks a dramatic shift in the pastor's sense of mutual calling; it demands that church leaders who seek stability devote as much attention to the professional satisfaction of the spouse as they give to supporting the clergy in leadership of the congregation.

The treasurer is the other figure who often dramatically uses his or her position to affect the length and effectiveness of a pastorate. Because of the small church's uncertainty of income and the continual need for hard work just to survive, one executive reported, "the treasurer often develops a protective stance that quenches any enthusiasm for new programs." Sometimes the treasurer represents a power figure who has a need to be in control, but often the treasurer could be more flexible if the entire congregation will help by removing the loneliness of his or her responsibility. The pastor cannot resolve this kind of financial conflict without involving more people from the congregation. Only an active membership can liberate an oppressed treasurer, but the pastor must help identify the problem and suggest options.

Program

Program "success" is the second most frequently mentioned source of tension between pastor and people of the small church. Sometimes this frustration is simply the inappropriate application of program norms that are suitable and appropriate for larger congregations, but can be oppressive for both the members and the pastors of small churches. We can see from FACT data that large churches do generate more programs, as expected. Further, although personal relationships are important in smaller churches (61 percent), in larger congregations they become a program necessity (85 percent). (Fig. 4a)

Pastors often express frustration at the number of people who are available to participate in any particular program. There is a "critical mass" of assembled people necessary for a program to feel "right" to the participants. There may not be enough women available for an association, or youth for a communicants class, or toddlers for a church-hour nursery. Or they are unpredictable, all coming at once then none at all.

Even if the participants could be found, pastors often feel that their churches lack the adults with proper training for leadership positions. "How can we have a Sunday school," laments one pastor,

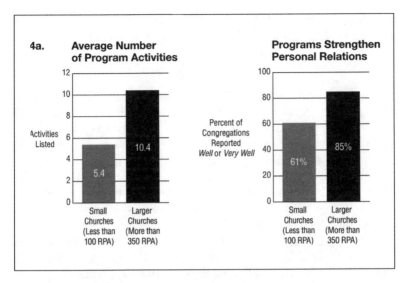

4a. **Average Number of Program Activities**

Activities Listed

Small Churches (Less than 100 RPA): 5.4

Larger Churches (More than 350 RPA): 10.4

Programs Strengthen Personal Relations

Percent of Congregations Reported *Well* or *Very Well*

Small Churches (Less than 100 RPA): 61%

Larger Churches (More than 350 RPA): 85%

"when we don't have any teachers?" Even with training, the teachers would be faced with materials designed for many small groups of homogeneous participants. Pastors usually have had their student training in larger churches, and lay leaders tend to be homegrown. Too often, the members feel inadequate and the pastor feels unappreciated.

Different measurements for the "success" of the program lie at the heart of the conflict, and leaders are far more aware that the hyperactivity can be as demoralizing as too few choices. Still, denominational reports tend to identify success with numbers. The annual membership report is only the most obvious pressure. The numerical inquiries seem endless: such as number of worshipers? Number of church-school classes, students, and teachers? Number of pledging units? Total income, special income, and benevolence income? Number of baptized babies, adults, and communicants? Number of marriages and funerals? In addition, there are the more subtle questions about programs, condensed into numbers: how many church groups? What kinds? Who comes? Using what materials? With what income and expense? The message is clear: the "effective church" is too often defined by program, program, and more program. The church may not be simply the number of people who attend on Sunday morning; but it is the sum of all its parts, the total of all its different activities. The pastor is a program pusher, hustler, perhaps huckster.[6] The "real" church has something for everyone. That is the burden of so many statistical reports.

Evaluating Success

A small, caring, single-cell church has a different definition for success. For a real program, everyone is present. An "almost real" program does not need to be attended by everyone, but all who are absent will hear about it before nightfall. When everyone participates in everything, pastors do not need to plan and push something different for each age group and interest center in the church. Such program divisions are seen as divisive by members of the caring cell. After a lifetime of hands-on experience and reflection, Douglas Alan Walrath has written an especially helpful guide that urges small church pastors to be "as practical as they are faithful."[7] As a contemporary challenge to small-church clergy, Walrath extends the meaning of practical leadership from personal caring to computer proficiency—the pastor does not need to do it all, just see that it all gets done.

These multiple definitions of success precipitate three kinds of problems for pastors of small churches: financial resources, human resources, and exhaustion.

- First, programs need money to support them, and materials to work with. There is a cost to the church whenever the building is opened, and a cost to the membership when trips are organized and materials are ordered. An energetic pastor may add as much as 25 percent to the cost of operating the church simply by promoting his well-meaning programs. When the treasurer asks about the source of funding for these programs, pastors sometimes feel that their leadership is being threatened. Program ideas become very personal. As one pastor complained when his hot-meals program was challenged on the grounds of fiscal feasibility, "They just didn't like my 'baby.' "
- Second, beyond the tangible financial resources, new programs also require an investment of human energy. Many times the new pastor will feel the need for new programs simply to prove that the church is alive. Old

members of the congregation may not feel the same urgency to prove their existence. One such pastor exploded at his official board: "Why do you vote for programs that you do not expect to personally support?" He accused them of apathy and hypocrisy, in the name of Jesus. Later one board member took him aside quietly and asked, "Is it hypocrisy or apathy, or is it Christian kindness to give you the permission to do what you have the desire and the energy to attempt? We were only trying to be helpful."

• Finally, when the tangible and human resources are expended, exhaustion follows. Sometimes effective leadership can inspire a flurry of activity. In a patient, loving way, many small churches have responded to the leadership of pastors who have called for a rich diversity of programs with something for everyone. They did it all. But when the young pastor receives the inevitable call to a place of greater responsibilities, they are exhausted. A time of quietness often follows a season of feverish activity.

One church executive who helps small churches in their search for pastors has become particularly sensitive to symptoms of exhaustion. He claims that he can predict the length of time a small congregation will take before they call the next pastor. He has calculated that the time between pastorates is directly related to the number of programs that the last pastor initiated: the more programs, the longer the interval. "The small church needs time for R & R, rest and recovery," he says. "They may not even assemble a pastor-nominating committee for a year or so, until the people are rested and ready." They are, says one observer, "burned-out."

Small-church programs can be enthusiastic and effective. But the programs must fit the style and character of the congregation. Some pastors seem to tune in more easily to the pace of the small congregation, with the rhythm of changing seasons and time for the needs of people. One Ohio pastor responded to a discussion of time in the pastorate by saying he was glad to have found the small-church ministry after serving in larger churches: "One of the things I like best is the pace. People don't look at their watches every few minutes during a conversation."

The Self-image of the Pastor

"The Pastor's Study and Professional Feelings," the exercise at the beginning of the chapter, provides an opportunity for pastors and members to "see their feelings" and examine the professional images that they project. Usually, the description of the pastor's study will suggest the ambivalence of our Christian calling: it is a personal workspace, but it is also an arena to share with other people. Usually, the pastor is surrounded by materials that support the program of the church: the desk, the bulletin board, the swivel chair, the telephone, perhaps a diploma, endless stacks of papers, and program supplies. The pastor is a program pusher, and the study is usually a workshop, a space for constructing programs.

In most pastors' studies, the visitor is kept at a distance. Typically, a large desk separates the pastor and the visitor. But often the barriers are more subtle, such as the size of the books (heavy and "important" looking) or the heights of the chairs (the pastor sits higher) or the glare of lights (the visitor looks toward the window).[8] The visitor may be impressed with pastor productivity, but put off by none-too-subtle symbols of clergy importance.

The same message may be seen in lists of satisfactions and frustrations that the clergy feel in their calling: most frustrations are related to unfinished work, interruptions, too much busywork, disorganization, and feelings of limited time and unlimited tasks. Like the atmosphere of the pastor's study, his or her frustrations reflect the pastor's concern for work to be done and schedules to be met. Clergy in smaller congregations have a shorter tenure than clergy of larger congregations, as suggested by the wide variety of congregations reporting in FACT data. (Fig. 4b) There are many reasons for this mobility, but longer tenures in smaller churches should include a sense of vocation and personal satisfaction.

Now examine the pastor's list of satisfactions. Typically, most of the satisfactions are in contrast to the office clutter and the pro-

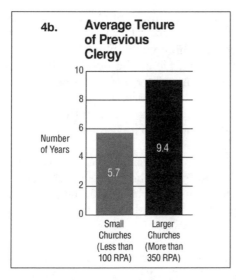

4b. Average Tenure of Previous Clergy

Number of Years

Small Churches (Less than 100 RPA): 5.7
Larger Churches (More than 350 RPA): 9.4

gram frustrations. For most small-church pastors, the satisfactions are overwhelmingly in the area of personal relationships. Typical satisfactions in-clude: working with people, sharing lives and crises, feeling loved and supported, preaching and pastoral calls, ministering to people, having a family and sharing family with others, and enabling people. Of course, some satisfactions are related to a job well done. Some frustrations include being too accessible.

But the contrast is consistent and striking: in the first three areas of his or her office— appearance of the office, the visitor's impression, and professional frustrations—the pastor has a self-image of one who constructs and pushes program. But in the satisfactions of a Christian vocation, the small-church pastor feels rewarded by personal relationships.

If that is the reward, then why are there so many tensions and role conflicts, not only with members, but primarily within the lives of the pastors themselves?[9] In the small church, many pastors have reflected on their misjudgments—that they have over-rated their power in changing the community, and underrated their importance in touching the lives of people.

When disagreeing with a leading member of the congregation, a pastor sometimes actually hears the famous line, "Reverend, I was here before you came (pause), and after you are gone, I will still be here." That is the classical definition of the continuity of power that holds the fort in many small churches. The pastor enters the situation as "servant of the servants of the Lord." Congregational leadership, which may appear to be apathetic toward outside intervention, has remarkable energy for maintaining the status quo. One student intern noted the delights of being "part of the family," but also observed the "fierce loyalty and determination" of the continuity of their Christian commitment.

The young pastor may confuse high visibility with leadership. The pastor is middle management. He or she does not own the store, but only manages it. Both the pastor and the congregation know that the store really belongs to the Lord, but the fabric of the congregation knows who owns the voting shares in the corporation. Some have identified the small-church pastor as a manager. (Although the large-church pastor is also a manager, in such a structured organizations the flow of decision-making is more transparent and more "rationalized.") In the small-church culture over time, the power of decisions may have gravitated to the treasurer, to the first sergeant of the Lord, or to the matriarch. Power may still be widely distributed among several families and significant people in the congregation. Power is not necessarily located in the church board, vestry, or council. As long as the pastor runs the store according to the established policies, power figures are willing to remain out of sight.[10] Raw power in the small congregation will surface when established procedures have been threatened or community values have been challenged, as we will consider in various chapters below. In this context, pastors have relational credit rather than organizational clout. In these settings, where a misunderstanding of power has created unnecessary tensions between pastors and people, pastors have access to a far more pervasive and satisfying leadership image, namely, "the lover."

The Pastor as Lover

Although members of small congregations want the benefit of skilled pastors to serve their churches, they place an even higher priority on having a pastor whom they feel they know personally. The most frequently mentioned frustration for the laity is the feeling that the well-trained pastor, hiding behind that professional polish, is not a real person. They want to know the person—that is their first priority.

As professional clergy, three styles of pastoral relationship may be identified: specialist, generalist, and lover. The person serving on the staff of a large congregation must function as a team player, a *specialist*. The same is true for any staff position in the denomination, the military, the hospital, or any other institution. Most advanced training is directed toward the improvement of the specialist's skills in ministry. To the specialist, personal life and relationships are secondary. The pastor might be friendly or distant; extroverted or withdrawn; married, single, or in transition. The staff member is employed for the particular skills he or she brings to the team.

However, if the congregation has only one professionally prepared person, then the pastor must be a *generalist*. The pastor is a one-person staff. He or she may not do everything equally well, but all dimensions of the organization must be covered. Generalists are measured by the strength of various programs throughout the church.

The small church cannot afford a specialist and is not primarily interested in measuring success based on program activity. The small church is built around the relationships of people to people. They want to know the pastor as a person, first. Only second are they interested in the pastor's skills. Members of the small church want from their pastor what they find most satisfying in belonging to the small church; they are not primarily interested in the specialist or the generalist. The small church wants a *lover*.

The image of lover should imply physical, but not sexual, connotations. Members of smaller congregations are more apt to be in touch with one another, physically as well as spiritually. The pastor embodies that sense of touching. In some churches, members want to touch the pastor in return. In other congregations, it is more reassuring to view the pastor as a loving father figure, austere but available. Whatever the general cultural norms, touching is more readily practiced in small churches. The pastor as lover is a source of stability, a kind of human Blarney Stone. There is no substitute for the presence of the pastor. He or she is the tangible symbol of love, the lover.

Professional skills seem to be a barrier that separates the people from the real person of the pastor.[11] Members of small churches have a curious method of reemphasizing the common humanity of the pastor. They enjoy his or her mistakes. They tell stories about the time the pastor stumbled into the pulpit, or made a slip of the tongue in preaching, or announced the wrong names in the midst of the funeral, or dropped the ring at the wedding, ad nauseam. To the educated pastor, who prides himself or herself on polished skills of ministry, these memories are humiliating. To the members, the stories underscore what they find most appealing about the pastor; he or she is a real person. The stories are intended not to criticize the pastor, but to bind pastor to people. Sometimes the pastor will enjoy the stories but the spouse will take offense.[12] The pastor's family that survives will learn that these stories are the lore of the village viewpoint which lead to the deepest kind of human acceptance. Rather than inhibiting the pastor, they are the liberating words that indicate that he or she has been accepted as a person. The pastor is free to be a character in the community.

Few young pastors are sufficiently at ease with themselves to enjoy the "liberation" to be human that the small church provides. Seminary education and denominational placement materials have taught them to value their specific, measurable skills. Evaluation of professional expertise continues throughout the pastor's career. Some small congregations have accepted the special ministry to help seminary graduates prepare for ministry in a very different way. They help them emphasize their humanity, to be pastoral lovers.

But how do you measure a lover? The pastor of a small congregation is often unprepared for the absence of feedback on professional skills, and the avalanche of emotional "stroking." The pastor of the small church cannot use the criteria of success that have been learned from seminary education or found in denominational reports. The small-church pastor has a different set of satisfactions: for example, there are fewer programs, but a higher percentage of the church membership at each. Small churches have fewer people in the congregation, but they can be known and loved in many more situations. There are fewer comments or critiques on the sermon, but more caring for the whole life of the pastor and family. The pastor who wants to keep attention focused only on his or her professional skills will complain that serving a small church "is like living in a fishbowl." The skills of ministry have not shielded the family from the full-time caring, and curiosity, of the congregation. When the pastor's spouse complains that there is no one to talk to, he or she usually means that nothing is confidential in the network of village connections, even in the city.

The pastor who feels a great need for constant and consistent measurement of achievements should not expect to find his or her calling satisfied by the strokes of a small congregation. But the pastor who finds reward in relationships with people—all sorts of people in all kinds of moods—should find love in the small church, and return love.[13]

As for a sense of achievement: on a Sunday morning when the elderly parishioner who has slept through worship thanks the pastor for the sermon, the pastor of a caring cell will respond appropriately, "I love you, too."

Suggestions for Further Reading

Burt, Steve E. and Hazel Ann Roper. *The Little Church that Could: Raising Small Church Esteem.* Valley Forge, Pa.: Judson Press, 2000.
Hands-on discussion of the central psychic-spiritual issue in small churches.

Cushman, James E. *Beyond Survival: Revitalizing the Small Church.* Parsons, W.Va.: McClain Print Co., 1981.
Historical context sets contemporary ministry in helpful perspective.

Savage, John S. *Listening and Caring Skills in Ministry: A Guide for Pastors, Counselors, and Small Groups.* Nashville: Abingdon Press, 1996.
Recovering the basics when we take too much for granted.

Walrath, Douglas Alan. *Making it Work: Effective Administration in the Small Church.* Valley Forge, Pa.: Judson Press, 1994.
Practical wisdom from a lifetime of research and consulting.

PART TWO

Belonging

"It just feels good to come here," said one elderly member who climbed the steps to the church, leaning on the arm of her middle-aged son. The man turned to his adolescent son and pointed, "I remember when we climbed that old maple tree when I was your age." The boy was not impressed. He whispered to his mother, "Do I have to stay here all day with Dad and Grandma?"

The caring cell of the small church is a natural cocoon for personal memories and shared experiences. For some people, the place evokes a feeling, and for others it brings back specific mental images. But for the uninitiated, the place of the caring cell may evoke boredom and frustration.

The richest resource of most small churches lies in the feelings about members now, and the memories of feelings that they have had in the past. Being in the place evokes responses worth remembering. Preserving those memories is important to the small church. Conserving the relationship between people, place, and happening is the contribution of many small churches to the pilgrimage of church members. Small churches are not against change. They simply feel that conserving the past has a priority.

The next three chapters suggest the importance of belonging in the life of most small congregations. They affirm the past as their source of identity in three ways:

Time is defined by significant memories of events that shape or have shaped the image and the expectations of the congregation.

Space becomes *special places* when experienced with important people who remain anchors to the past or guides to the future.

Annual events and *personal passages* remind a caring cell of the length and breadth of God's concern throughout their lives and beyond.

History is the strength of the small church. Conserving these experiences can provide the energy for continuing ministry and mission.

Congregational Time Line

Developing a time line of congregational history is an opportunity for a major social and spiritual event, not only for the hardcore members, but also for sharing with younger and newer members alike. Working together to tell the significant stories in your congregation's history can provide vital insight into the almost unconscious values that have held you together and insight into the often unspoken hopes that keep you going.

Before the event, post a long sheet of newsprint or butcher paper on the wall, marking off the relevant years at the top, perhaps in decade intervals, and enter the names of pastors at the appropriate dates of their tenure (if they served the church more than briefly). Your time line should date back to the organizing of your congregation, since the shadow of the early years can stretch long across succeeding generations, and you should give some discussion in broad strokes to each succeeding era. But primary emphasis should be placed on the living memory of the church in the last half century.

You might begin by inviting all present to initial the time line at a point corresponding to the time of their earliest memories of your congregation. Along the top of the news-print, note the public events that impact congregational life (such as wars and depression, local calamities like fires and floods, civic events like a new courthouse or population shifts). Throughout the exercise, encourage participants to tell stories about their memories of the congregation at various points in its history. Invite someone from the congregation to make brief notes on the time line about the important events and descriptions your members offer. As the time line develops, ask members to recall:

- What traditions or activities were favorites, and why?

- Who were the leaders and "characters" of the congregation?

- What do they recall about worship, and about the people who lead it?

- What were the crises, and how did people pitch in?

- What were the disagreements in the church and community; how did they turn out?

- What was the congregation best known for, and how has that changed?

Reserve time at the end to get an overview of your time line. Try to identify three or four seasons or chapters in your congregational history, and name them. Make a short list of values or characteristics that have held your church together through all your struggles, and celebrate these in prayer and perhaps a closing song.

You may want to leave the time line on the wall, inviting people who missed the event to share their own stories. Members often enrich their time lines with pictures or other memorabilia. The event should be fun for old-timers and newcomers alike, and the follow-up should incorporate others into your story.[1]

Memory and Ministry

Belonging Is a Feeling

Belonging to a small church is a feeling. It is based on being among people who know you and among whom you feel at home. Members have lived their faith together. They have celebrated their separate victories and shared their individual losses together in the same place, and before the same Father God. They have learned what to expect from one another, and when to expect it. In effect, if Carol Perkins is late and Sam Riley is loud, then all is right with the world, because that's the way they are. People are who they are, although we may not know how to explain it, or even consciously remember to expect it. But Mr. Jones's question about the budget is as predictable as Sue Palokowski's singing off-key. "God love 'em, that's the way they are."

The caring church does not treat each person equally. We know one another too well. Each person is accepted, not equally, but individually by name.[2] Each person has a contribution to make and needs to be met. The caring church will tend to emphasize the uniqueness of each person.

In the caring community, the individual receives his or her name. Naming is formalized in baptism, but nicknames just happen. Everyone has a name. People may be named by a skill they display, by an event in their life, or even by a distinguishing physical characteristic. The local merchant who served in the war may be known as "Major" for the rest of his life. The tall boy may grow up with the handle of "Shorty." The old man may still be called

"Junior" long after his father has died. The woman who gets divorced may stay divorced in the minds of many long after she has remarried and moved away. People are remembered individually, intimately, and sometimes in awkward ways.[3]

Like the love of God in the old hymn, the caring cell has a "love that will not let me go." How many young pastors have first discovered the nature of the caring congregation when they tried to clean the rolls of the church? The enthusiastic cleric might suggest that the church council adopt objective criteria for membership, such as current participation, or recent contribution, or annual communion. He or she may even buttress his or her recommendation with a statement of official church policy. But before the list of "lost" members has been read very far, the church officers will balk because, "Well, around here things are not that clear-cut." Later, when a removed member reappears, the pastor may have to relive the story of the prodigal son, cast in the part of the angry elder brother. And if the prodigal member should die while still "in a far country," the church family members may announce correctly that "he was bone of our bone, and flesh of our flesh—always one of our own."

The small congregation remembers its own. Here they were named before God, and here they will be laid to rest, or at least will be mourned in their passing. The significant events in the life of the congregation are recorded "before God and these witnesses," as we remind ourselves in the liturgy for marriage. Here individuals have prayed in personal crises, and celebrated in times of joy. Collectively, as in the time line event, the congregation remembers the experiences that they shared, carefully stored away in memory, like "the afternoon we burned the mortgage," or "those picnics when we worshiped in the park." Significant people are remembered by their impact on the lives of others. Events are dated by the pastor who served at that time, if the pastor was more than "passing through."

In a personal way, the small church is the place where intimate memories are recalled. A formal church history might be published in a book, with accurate narrative and well-peopled photographs. But each person has an unprinted album of personal memories of church-school classmates and well-intentioned teachers, of prayer groups and mischief, of club meetings and very private meditations. These memories are not bound by the mind in order of appearance, but they are triggered by clues scattered throughout the building and the people, mingled with memories of "how it used to be here" and the rites of passages that are shared with a strange assortment of close friends and distant relations. Worship is a time of remembering, even without consciously considering the past.

In a broader sense, the small church is the carrier of experience with the Christian culture.[4] The transcendent and eternal God has been felt in this place, among these people. God has touched the members through the moments of celebration, or in the posture of prayer, or through hands that are gentle and arms that hold, in the smells of down-home cooking and the hush of the last to leave. Time is remembered, not as hands of the clock or squares of the calendar: time is remembered as Christian people who cared.[5] One student pastor in a caring congregation said it very simply with pained honesty: "Small churches look inward, rather than outward. They look backward, rather than forward."

Exceptions to History

History is a strength in most small congregations. They find themselves by looking inward and backward. This statement alone may be offensive to some pastors, and inappropriate to some congregations. History is a resource that is not available to many larger and younger congregations, and it is rejected as a resource by the future-oriented theology of some pastors.

Some congregations are newly organized in new and growing communities. They have a future to build on together, but they have no past that is uniquely their own. The innovation and creativity of most young congregations is nourished by the many Christian histories that the members weave together from other experiences in the faith. They build the new from the old.

Social mobility increases the importance of history, even as it makes a sense of history more difficult. One suburban pastor complained, "I have only been here two years, and we have not been able to grow; but of the two hundred people in my congregation, only forty were members when I came." Such congregations may have difficulty in establishing a firm sense of history. Yet they often desire it. Many areas of high mobility are composed of transients searching for an institution that will offer them a sense of belonging. Mobility may simply speed up the development and turnover of tradition, not deny its importance. "Our contribution," said a pastor in a changing urban area, "is to help people learn that the church was where they were, is where they are, and will be where they are going. They need us to be here, before they come and after they go."

When churches move, history may be more of a problem than when people move. When the population moves, the church offers a history in that place. But when the congregation relocates, its history may be out of context. The social history of a congregation may become a barrier for the congregation to reach the community. Some congregations are regional in character and draw from a larger area. But neighborhood congregations that move to a new place of worship have the same problems in merging with the community that other churches have in merging with one another.[6]

Some churches, and especially some pastors, deny the theological importance for a congregation to claim its history, or for a person to ever look back. For some, the rebirth experience in Christ opens the future but closes the past: "He who has put his hand to the plow. . . . " For others, the mission of the church is so absorbing that there is no time for yesterday or even today. This is a strange combination of those who talk about "conversion" and those who focus on causes—both aim to bring in the kingdom without building on the past. But time, in the Christian faith, is bigger than the future.

Biblical Memory

Our faith is based on memory. When defining the meaning of the faith-experience, or describing the qualities of God, our faith reaches back to the experience of God's people in the biblical record. According to biblical theologians, Israel knew God because the people remembered the great acts of God: "Of this group of 'events,' the call and promises to the fathers, the deliverance from slavery, and the gift of the land (the conquest) are known from liturgy and confessions to be the key elements of the whole story."[7] The faith of the people is placed in the faithfulness of God. What they remember determines what they believe about the future. What God has done in the past, God will do in the future. "Remember, O Israel, the Lord Your God, the Lord is One." Ours is a faith of remembering.

G. Ernest Wright points to this sense of history as being distinctively Christian: Christianity among the religions seems to be the only one that takes history seriously, for it assumes that the knowledge of God is associated with events that really happened in human life.[8] "The biblical point of view was to take history and historical tradition seriously and through them to foresee a future. Faith is thus set within the forms of history."[9]

Above all, Christians remembered. Peter remembered his promises broken and Christ's promises kept. The church remembered the new covenant "in remembrance of him." They remembered the images of the cross in the ground and the stone rolled away from the tomb. They remembered the Resurrection every first day of every week, Sunday. They remembered the gift of the Holy Spirit, and they remembered the words of our Lord. Faith is the memory of those who have proceeded us, the great cloud of witnesses, who walked this way before us. They remembered events: when Christianity begins to speak of the suffering of God, it speaks of the body language of God's suffering, the cross. When it speaks of deliverance, it speaks of an event, the Exodus. Whereas much popular religion is narrowly concerned with *ideas* about God and religion, the biblical witness remains more concerned with *events* in which the truth is historically embodied.

Throughout the centuries, Christians have shared in the biblical memory. History is not just part of our past, but we are part of that unfolding drama of faith. The roots of our Christian experience are a tangled mat of biblical witness and personal experience. Thus, Wright calls faith the "confessional recital of the redemptive acts of God in a particular history," where history includes "not only the events of seeming impersonal significance, but also the lives of the individuals who compose it."[10] The story unfolds in the lives of all of us, and in the lives of the congregations where we share and serve the Lord. For some congregations, memory has been their strength and inspiration. For others, the weight of the past has become a millstone and a source of despair. Christian memory can be used or abused.

Abuses of Memory

Many of the negative observations concerning the small church can be traced to bad memory—that is, the abuse of memory—in the caring cell. "Old," "closed," "ingrown," "ultraconservative," "prejudiced," "independent," "disconnected," "oligarchical," and "hung up on the past" are all descriptions that relate to an abuse of history in a congregation. Some history can be a burden, and some can be oppressive. One pastor from New Jersey said: "Our building is not old; it is simply run down. The congregation feels like the church looks—not old, but tired."

Memory can be a burden. The families that once were the strength of the congregation can become its liability. A young pastor in the South commented: "Family hostility blocks communication in our church. Often groups have rigid lines, and people live separated in their little boxes." Memories can divide the congregation—who joined under which pastor. The collective memory of the congregation can become a barrier to the inclusive church, what Lyle Schaller has called the "liturgical-ethnic-nationality-language-cultural-socioeconomic barrier."[11] What is nostalgia for some people may be nausea for others.

Memory can evoke feelings of guilt and grief for the good old days, especially if the congregation has "deteriorated." Of course, the good old days may never have been so good (most sanctuaries reflect the overoptimistic projections of a growth that never happened). But they are past, and therefore not as traumatic as the crises of the passing moment. The older members are often saddened by the memories. But the middle generation, the present church officers, often feel guilty that they cannot equal the feats of the past—even if conditions have changed. Those who grieve may be more flexible than those who feel guilty about the past as compared to the present situation.

Memory can be a means of avoiding the present. Some small churches have an "edifice complex." The community has changed, the members have moved away, and the building is the only familiar landmark left in the community. One consultant told me: "My work with marginal churches taught me that these Christians have to face a ministry that is not rooted in the past. . . . We must not crucify small churches, but we also must not unduly coddle them."

In all these ways, memory can be a burden, a source of guilt and sadness, and a way to avoid the problems of the present. But there is power in remembering. Memory can stir people emotionally far deeper than reason will allow. As one impatient executive observed, "Now that you have opened Pandora's box [by exploring the histories of congregations], how can the recollection of personal and congregational past be harnessed to the ministry of the present and the mission of the future?"

Dynamics of Memory

Small congregations lean toward denominational heritage, and are more likely to purchase denominational materials, according to FACT data. (Fig. 5a) Historical consciousness is a gift of God. At the deepest level, memory is the biblical affirmation of what God has done in our lives. We stand in the lineage of our faith when "we remember the Lord's death until he comes again."[12] God has touched us, individually and as his people, through particular people and in particular places. We have experienced the mighty acts of God. In this heritage, we are joined with the whole communion of the saints, past and future. Heritage, as FACT data suggests (Fig. 5a), is important for smaller congregations, as reflected in the affirmations of identity and in their (perhaps surprising) tenacity in supporting denominational publishers.

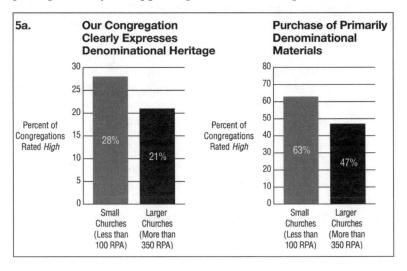

95

Individually, memory offers us distance from the pressure of any particular moment. In congregations with at least three generations represented (although rarely in the same families), the middle generation usually carries the burden of daily church work and management. They may assume that there is a "right way" to carry certain traditions, and to perform certain functions. The older generation has the perspective of memory: they remember that "we did not always do it this way when Mr. Hardy was pastor." Memory liberates through perspective and contrast.

In a strange way, even memory offers perspective on itself. By remembering, we can sort out of our experience what was relevant to that moment and what is of enduring value. Memory allows us to affirm the positive values of caring for people without becoming an advocate for a rural simplicity or an ethnic "old country" that has no basis in current reality. Memory allows us to select from our past that experience which is useful in the present.

Memory also recalls images and models of the past that inspire us in the face of immediate problems. The chairperson of the building campaign can remind the congregation of those "twenty-seven courageous founders in faith who first laid the cornerstone for this church." Fund-raising, evangelism, social concern, teaching church school—all can be inspired by the memory of those who have "gone on before us," who have "touched us with their love," who have "made this place possible."

Memory is the strongest motive for ministry in the small cell of caring Christians. Wright suggests that the power of memory is embedded in the gospel: "An integral part of the proclamation is the apostles themselves as witnesses of the event, a feature which contains in embryo the later insistence that the ministry is an integral part of the gospel story."[13] As we have been touched by love, so we feel moved to touch the lives of others.

Conversely, the most offensive insult to most proud congregations is the suggestion that the members have betrayed their heritage. One student intern observed that the strongest motivation in the small church was the "fear of letting the church down." Or for a friend to say, "I never would have thought that of *you*," is a criticism that stirs the caring cell to response, sometimes with deep feelings.

Memory is more than a recitation of the past as it really was. What we "choose" to remember may be our deepest longings for what will unfold in the future. Our past is a mixture of dreams and fears, never what it really was. Our memory tells us more about who we are than who we were, more about our hopes and fears for the future than what really happened in the past.

As in the ancient myth, hope is the last of the spirits that we almost left in Pandora's box. Hope can be released by the positive memory of the congregation. The storytellers in the congregation are no less important than the planners in shaping the future of the congregation. Churches can attempt only what they can imagine. Memory grows with new experience, and tradition builds on significant events. Storytellers who remember events through the eyes of courage and hope can turn memory into even stronger ministry.

Using Memories for Ministry

One surprise in the past quarter century is the enthusiastic discovery of this historical consciousness as a foundational resource to help congregations move into the future. In a climate dominated by organizational consultants who urged "envisioning your future" and "manage by objectives," church leaders discovered the importance of knowing where they are going by remembering where they came from. "Unlike medieval or ancient peoples, moderns have to labor at identifying who they are," writes James P. Wind in a book dedicated to helping congregations rediscover their identity through defining their history.[14] As members identify their faith roots in their own stories of earlier years, they grow in confidence to deal with current issues. One seaside consultant explained, "It's like rowing a boat—to know where you are going, you have to see where you have been."

- *From Spiritual Vitality to Program Planning*: Preaching and worship have most easily incorporated the stories of struggle and strength of local heroes into the regular patterns and rich consciousness of congregational life.[15] We might not have anticipated how to help translate these spiritual roots in congregational history into creative new program possibilities. In what they call a "strategic and spiritual approach" to church planning, Alban Institute consultants Roy M. Oswald and Robert E. Friedrich, Jr., map out an integrated sequence to discern congregational values and mobilize spiritual energies for all sizes of congregations. The mid-point and most participatory aspect of this sequence is a congregational event to develop a time line for ministry assessment, instructing participants to "involve congregants in the excitement of the ancient art of storytelling. Collectively piece together *your story*." [16]

- *Recruiting New Members and Volunteers:* The time line produces more than shared memories. In real people living through tough times, this historical event brings the ministry of the church to life. When the old stories are dusted off and retold, new members can be incorporated into the fabric of the congregation. If the emotions are real, people from different generations cross age barriers in the authenticity of experience. If the past struggles reflect significant contributions that the church has made in the lives of its members, it improves the climate in which volunteers are more likely to step forward to continue and expand God's ministry in that place. Sometimes these events evolve moments of congregational recognition for members who have had a special impact in the church and its community of concern. When they are recognized, the whole community is stronger.[17]

- *More Alumni, New Resources:* As the "characters" are remembered when the stories are retold, the small church increases its informal network even without expanding its formal membership. In their history, small congregations are in touch with far more people, and the feelings of belonging sink deeper into those who share the memories. With a larger network and increased commitment, the line between members, "alumni," and "friends of the church" becomes blurred, and together they can uncover a wide variety of unexpected ways to expand their support for the small-church ministry. Congregational identity through history does not magically transcend the financial limitations of small-membership church. But participants who take pride in their heritage and traditions are more likely to support their congregation financially and to find other support in new and imaginative ways.

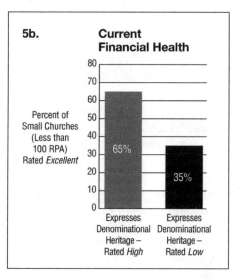

5b. **Current Financial Health**

Percent of Small Churches (Less than 100 RPA) Rated *Excellent*

65%

35%

Expresses Denominational Heritage – Rated *High*

Expresses Denominational Heritage – Rated *Low*

- *Financial Strength*: Those findings in FACT data (Fig. 5b) are consistent with the recommendations of Anthony Pappas, who argues that "the first strategy of successful fund-raising in the small church is to utilize the concern for the well-being of the congregation."[18] Pappas proceeds to invert and reinterpret various negative aspects of small congregations (including those mentioned here and in the previous chapters) as resources for strengthening financial support in small congregations. In his list of bad aspects made good, he includes habits, accidents, crises, intimacy, counter-cultural attitudes and even nostalgia, all of which can be converted into assets for a congregation that knows its history, cares about its turf, and believes that, in faith, God can work miracles. These efforts do not convert the small church into a larger congregation in miniature.

In every congregation, change depends on the right
sense of timing.

Catching the Beat

Pace, or timing, is basic to the character of most congregations.
For many young pastors, pacing is the most difficult dimension of
belonging in the caring cell. If a young pastor who has the energy
of a sprinter is located in a small congregation with the grace of a
distance runner, the result may be a brief pastorate.

The pace of a caring cell may be heard in the rhythm of the
hymns, and the timing of the anthem. It is reflected in the cadence
of speech, seen in the ambling of unrushed people, noticed in the
time it takes for called meetings to get down to business. People-
time can be measured (if anyone cares) in the length of time after
the benediction until the sanctuary is empty (in reverse proportion to the number of worshipers), or the length of time between
the arrival of the first pot for the covered-dish supper and the
beginning of the evening program, if indeed something has been
planned. People-time dominates many small congregations and
frustrates many "program-time pastors."

In the rhythm of calendar days, Sunday provides a rest beat.
Sunday is the sacred hour when the caring cell gathers to reaffirm
their faith in God, and their contact with one another. The style,
length, content, and choreography of worship all confirm the
members' pilgrimage with one another and their contact with the
seasons of the earth.[19] Pace is important. As one pastor lamented,
"They will remember the length of the sermon much longer and
more accurately than they can recall what I said."

The church-school experience is part of the rhythm of the passing seasons. One teacher complained that "the curriculum material is too educational, and not Christian enough." She did not
mean that it was too complex, or even too finely graded. She was
concerned that the basic, simple values that she communicated to
her children were obscured in the many alternative readings of
the biblical text. The small church lives on people-time, which
recruits teachers. As one pastor said, "They are religious, that is
they come regularly every week, with more preparation of the
soul than work on their lesson." The primary lesson of Sunday

school is to *feel* the sustaining love of the eternal God, mediated in memorable *people and places*.

For many small churches, the time line is not a rearview mirror to the past. Rather it's the best of who we are, warts and all, and that, by God's grace, will carry us into the future.

Suggestions for Further Reading:

Anderson, Herbert, and Edward Foley. *Mighty Stories, Dangerous Rituals: Weaving Together the Human and the Divine.* San Francisco: Jossey-Bass, 1998.

Story and ritual combined explain the power of small church faith-practices.

Burt, Steve. *Activating Leadership in the Small Church: Clergy and Laity Working Together.* Valley Forge, Pa.: Judson Press, 1988.

How clergy can help members share the leadership load of small churches.

Oswald, Roy M., and Robert E. Friedrich, Jr. *Discerning Your Congregation's Future: A Strategic and Spiritual Approach.* Bethesda, Md.: Alban Institute, 1996.

Organizational planning approach that fits small church sensibilities.

Pappas, Anthony. *Money, Motivation and Mission in the Small Church.* Valley Forge, Pa.: Judson Press, 1989.

Helping small church leaders turn financial limits into spiritual strength.

The Silent History of the Church

Things accumulate meaning and value as they become associated with important events and significant people in our lives. A "silent history" of the congregation can be developed by identifying and, where possible, assembling the objects that have historical significance.

Begin with the place of worship, the sanctuary. The most obvious objects will be found in or associated with the gathering of the congregation. Some of the most important objects may be unmovable or out of sight.

Next, move through the rooms and grounds of the church in search of things that have meaning to the members. Some things are immediately attractive; others are significant because it would "cause a fight" to try to move it or change it.

Further, there are some hidden places to look for the silent history. Church closets are often a gold mine of memorabilia—things that had too much meaning to throw out but are too unkempt to display. Soon they will be simply junk. Sometimes the closets of former pastors and retired church officers will yield a treasure that captures the essence of a particular moment in the history of the congregation. Last, there's the kitchen: some of those old pots and quaint serving dishes have a story to tell.

The silent history can be woven into a historical narrative of the congregation that can fascinate the children and remind the old-timers. Through the silent history, the congregation is literally in touch with the past.

CHAPTER SIX

Places of Ministry

Places are important because of the memories we have of the people who have shared experiences with us, and the memories are rooted in particular places. In a world where some pursue an insatiable hunger for endless space, theologian Walter Brueggemann gives voice to the biblical claim to rootedness.

> Place is space which has historical meanings, where some things have happened which are now remembered and which provide continuity and identity across generations. Place is space in which important words have been spoken which have established identity, defined vocation, and envisioned destiny. Place is space in which vows have been exchanged, promises have been made, and demands have been issued. Place is indeed a protest against the unpromising pursuit of space. It is a declaration that our humanness cannot be found in escape, detachment, absence of commitment, and undefined freedom.[1]

One local church leader explained it in particularly dramatic terms, saying, "Places have ghosts of the people who have used them. I can never worship without remembering—or enter the choir room without 'seeing' a welcome face." Most of us, although not so graphic in our imagination, have felt the tug of particular places where we have been touched by others and by the presence of the Lord.

Places become important far beyond their material replacement value. Congregations still meet in dilapidated buildings that are sometimes dangerous and even officially condemned. The casual observer must wonder at the rationality of people who cling to the old place, especially when they could move to newer facilities nearby. Commitments to space come not from the mind, but from the heart. The church building may be mortgaged and in need of repairs, but, said an urban pastor, "This place is a landmark in a sea of change, and a source of stability to many who never attend." Even highly mobile Americans carry the memories of precious places wherever they go, eliciting a greater nostalgic need for roots among those who seem to have the least.[2]

Biblical Affirmations

Widely different theological streams are joined at one point: the importance of place in discerning and doing the Word of God. Theologies of liberation, with their emphasis on the need for change, and theologies of conservation, with their assurances of continuity, both join in their affirmation of a God who speaks to real people in particular places. Paul Tournier has put the case:

> How are we to reconcile our need both for a universal and for a personal God? It seems to me that the Bible gives a clear answer. The God of the Bible is indeed a universal God, but he is a God who nevertheless chooses places in which to reveal himself to men [and women] .... He ... chooses particular meeting-places in order to make contact with men.[3]

The relationship between people and the earth is acknowledged in the description of Creation and gift of the Garden of Eden. The call of Abraham and the covenants of Israel with God must be seen in the context of the promised *land*. The covenant at Mt. Sinai provides guidelines for service in the land, promised to the fathers, to be passed on to their children. Early prophets warned about the loss of the land, and later prophets in exile looked forward to the return to the land where God will in fact be king. For Jeremiah, the first symbol of the new covenant was the purchase of land in the face of the enemy. The land where "we have known the Lord" is the foundation of Old Testament faith.

But the land is more than the deserts of Sinai or the cities of Palestine. In the New Testament, the relationship of power and the kingdom are central to the good news of Jesus. In response to the proclamation and person of Jesus, the cornerstone of faith is the commitment to a particular group in a specific place. Jesus both touched the lives of particular people, and challenged the assumptions of wealth and the corruptions of power. His message only had effect when the Spirit moved particular people to share their lives in ministry together. Walter Brueggemann summarizes: "The central (biblical) problem is not emancipation but *rootage*, not meaning but *belonging*, not separation from community but *location* within it, not isolation from others but *placement* deliberately between the generation of promise and fulfillment. The Bible is addressed to the central human problem of homelessness (anomie)."[4]

When Place Is Sacred

Nothing in my seminary education prepared me for the importance of place in the growth of the believer to become an instrument of God's love. I learned this dimension of faith from a patient parishioner in a time of personal grief. After her husband of forty years had died two months earlier, she had spent a quiet time with her sister in another community. One Sunday she returned, came into the sanctuary late "to avoid too many friends," and found that her pew was occupied by a young couple who had begun to attend in her absence. The following Saturday she came to visit me. As a widow she wanted help with what she called "my sin of idolatry." She went on to explain: "For thirty-eight years I shared that pew with my husband. I know it is idolatrous, pastor, but I feel God is *closer* to me there than anywhere else. There is no place like that pew on earth."

On Saturday, we left my study to sit in the pew together, and we were both literally touched by the place. On Sunday, she shared it with the young couple, and with their squirming child. She shared the pew and her memories. The young couple "took up residence" just a pew away. They became very close to the older woman and to the ministry of that church.

Her experience provides a model for many small congregations who want to reach out but do not know how. They have a sense of God in a place that is precious to them. But they do not know how to share that experience with others. Many pastors have expressed the dilemma: "My folks are very interested in their own doings. But they couldn't care less about what goes on in the community." A church officer in a farming area said: "All our energy is consumed in surviving. We have nothing left to reach out into the community." For both of these situations, the key to service is found in the importance of place.

The widow used her pew in two ways, to reach the pastor and then the young couple. First, she invited them to share it physically, and they sat together. Second, she let its meaning touch them spiritually when she told them her story of sharing her pew in her church with them. Both the pastor and the young couple were changed by the experience. In the act of caring, in sharing her place, the woman found herself healed as well.

Place is important in the caring cell. Here we have been touched, and here we remember. But that place will lose its importance if others are not permitted to share the experience. Ministry through a place will touch people in two ways. It touches those who find a place, as in the case of the pastor and the young couple. It touches those who care, as it did the widow. Paul Tournier, who is a psychotherapist as well as a theologian, says: "The giving of a place to those who have none seems to me to be one way of defining our vocation as healers of persons. As we have seen, one becomes a person only if one really has a place. So in helping our patients to find their places we are helping them to become persons."[5] Small churches have in abundance the gifts that Paul Tournier says are essential for healing others: they know who they are, and they have a place to share.

Healing Ministries

Healing ministries can be seen in churches that state their particularity. "We are who we are," they say in effect. "We are the community church," says one suburban pastor, "and we want the community to share our building even if they are not members of the congregation." The emphasis is placed on reaching and serving a particular community, or a particular segment of the urban population. One urban pastor explained: "I emphasize the geographical parish; we are the church of this neighborhood. That reduces the threat of being overwhelmed by confining the size of our concern."

Healing ministries focus on one specific human need. As many pastors note, "We have learned to personalize the issues." Members respond to help people as people. Usually, they do not wait to form a committee and get everything organized. Often they do not trust organization, even if they know the people in the local government bureaucracy or the church denominational hierarchy. Even if such human structures would work, they would not seem to be as much fun. One woman said, "We help first and plan later—if necessary."

Pastors often seem to be attracted to the larger issues and the conceptual questions of social policy. Some pastors put their faith in planned community change. The pulpit is used by some pastors to enunciate these larger questions.

Small-church ministries may accidentally precipitate significant changes in community services. In faith, they may move mountains, or at least nudge the power pyramids of their communities. But social change is not their intention or ambition. They simply care about people.

Ministries most frequently found working in and through small congregations are related to care in times of crises in people's lives. Usually, as a result of a problem of someone in the church or in their community, a congregation will discover the inadequate care available to anyone who is caught in a crisis. In response, such congregations have begun food pantries and soup kitchens, cash assistance and clothing banks. In time, they may expand to programs of rehabilitation for addiction to drugs, alcohol, and gambling, mental health clinics, upgraded community services, and even heifer projects overseas. But the spark is personal, and the human need is physical. From FACT data, note how congregations support a safety net for personal and family crises by providing money, food, and clothing in emergencies. By comparison with larger congregations, note the very high percentage of small churches that are using a far greater proportion of their meager resources to respond to neighbors in need. (Fig. 6a)

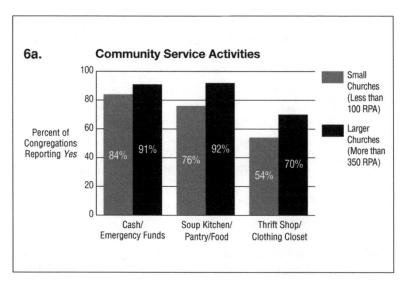

6a. Community Service Activities

Percent of Congregations Reporting *Yes*

Small Churches (Less than 100 RPA)

Larger Churches (More than 350 RPA)

Cash/Emergency Funds: 84%, 91%
Soup Kitchen/Pantry/Food: 76%, 92%
Thrift Shop/Clothing Closet: 54%, 70%

Typical is the experience reported by a small church in Ohio. Through a crisis in one family in the community, members of the church discovered the gaps in the government welfare program. A food pantry was established, but it was quickly wiped out. The pastor reports: "Our church officers had to swallow their pride when it was obvious that the church could not do the job alone. We had to be a stopgap caregiver. We could not run "our church program," but we would have to fit ourselves in with government resources and other churches in our area. The ministry has helped nonmembers realize that the church does care for them." But the greatest effect has been upon the church. "Members have lost their preconceived notion of mission and have begun a ministry to those in need—a natural mission, and it feels good."

Similar stories could be told of many congregations that have responded to particular people in need. The needs of senior citizens often attract the attention of the congregation. Churches have developed nutrition programs and meals-on-wheels; they have adopted nursing homes and helped elderly people go shopping. Prayer groups and Bible study often bring the elderly together in otherwise dismal conditions. Sometimes it pays off. At least one congregation has funded its entire social ministry through the semiannual sale of "Handmade Articles and Homemade Goodies" prepared by the elderly for whom the program was developed.

Child care is another concern that has found a place in many small congregations, especially day care, nursery schools, and classes for children with learning disabilities. Other churches provide help for youth, for distraught parents, and even for those who want to grow flowers and vegetables in the midst of the city.

"This Is Love—Pass It On"

The fact remains that many small churches do not have any noticeable social ministry. They are concerned only with their own doings. They believe that they have given all their energy for survival, and have nothing left for a social ministry. One church dropout complained that the church will not last when "the will to survive is more important than its capacity to care for people—that's self-defeating."

What is the difference between those who generate programs of community ministry and those who do not? The difference is not found in the number of members, or any of the resources that can be counted, such as money, mortgage, or the ages of members. The difference lies in the attitude of the members.

Small churches with healing ministries have four attitudes in common:

- First, they take a Christian pride in the kind of faith that has been passed on to them. They have been touched by love, and remember how important it was for them. By the grace of God, they feel a special satisfaction in passing that love on to others. The storytellers recount times of crises, and how the congregation came through in emergencies. Legends about the founders include examples of generous gifts and whispering of secret support for those in special need. Caring for others is considered essential to the character of the congregation.
- Second, in specific ministries of healing, they respond to a person in need, not to a community survey. As one analyst observed, "Interest followed action." When the need is evident, the congregation responds. The inclination to respond is supported by the matriarchs and

patriarchs, and is facilitated by a caring pastor. The pastor cares enough to allow the members to respond. The pastor does not short-circuit the request and preempt the opportunity for others to respond, but rather finds the people who are most interested and the ways that are most helpful.

- Third, the people of the congregation show that they own their space together, not individually.[6] In most cases, they share in the maintenance: members have painted the community room, stitched the curtains, and repaired the concrete walk. The place belongs to everyone for the purpose of sharing, because it is the House of the Lord. Like the land of the biblical promise, it is theirs for service, to pass on.
- Fourth, the congregation acknowledges their debt to those who have come before. They appreciate what they have inherited. For older congregations, this appreciation is often associated with objects that have historical meaning. For younger churches, it is often reflected in commitment to the broader programs of the denomination. Churches with a healing ministry usually are the first to say that they are just passing on the love they have received from others.

Silent History

The exercise in silent history at the beginning of this chapter is a way to lift up our feelings and acknowledge our debt to those who have preceded us. Assembling and honoring the artifacts of history makes our faith seem tangible, even to the youngest in our Christian family. Faith has always found powerful things through which to focus meaning and pass it on from believer to believer, from one generation to the next. The Lord's Supper uses common objects not as a concession to our humanity, but as an affirmation that God has touched us through the particular and mundane elements of life. The cross has been raised over the centuries as a physical representation that points beyond itself, embracing all people, yet located in a particular time and place.

The silent history does not make the objects holy or sacred in their own right. Like all memorials, the symbolic things that point beyond themselves are a way of showing our appreciation to the sacrifice and contribution of those who have proceeded us. Memorials are not shrines, but simply a way of saying thanks to people who made the present possible.

In silent history, most attention usually is given to the things that are associated with people in the sanctuary: the pulpit, the Bible, and the vessels of communion, in that order. Personal relationships are recalled in things that make music—organ, chimes, bells, and piano. Many people also remember the windows, the pews, pastor's chair, and even the lighting of the chandelier. But strangely, few adults have mentioned either the cross or the doors, unless these items are architecturally unique.

Outside the sanctuary, consensus declines rapidly. Often there are pictures and lists of people, framed and well remembered. Pastors' pictures are often treasured, the "gallery of old goats," as one teenager fondly noted. There are often specific objects that draw the attention of some: the "gathering oak" tree in the front lawn, the cemetery to the side, the furnace "that we once stoked by hand." Many people mention the wall plaques that specifically say "in appreciation" to unknown members of former generations. The names may not be known, but the sense of gratitude is widely shared.

Exorcising Places

Silent history is satisfying to prepare and widely appealing in its presentation. But it can do more for a church than merely provide for a museum in the narthex. By honoring our history, we can satisfy our need to say thanks to the past. When we have recognized the meaning that some places have for some people, then we can liberate those rooms for other uses.

As long as we ignore the "ghosts" that inhabit particular rooms in the memories of many members, we will not be permitted to use those rooms for anything that might offend their shadow occupants. The silent history can be expanded to include the stories that the walls could tell. Each room in the church has a history, a narrative of the events that have been sheltered and embraced in that particular place. Old rooms can be exorcised by telling their stories, by respecting the meaningful memories of that room for members of the church. Even better, the meaning of the room can be most fully liberated if an object that symbolizes the events of that place can be honored in the sight of all. Even the kitchen can be freed of restraints when the ghosts of dedicated service are granted the respect and rest they deserve.

Making Sacred Places Portable

Spaces and objects become sacred as they are associated with a significant moment in our lives, and a sense of divine presence. Congregations may lift up particular artifacts, or even the whole sanctuary, as a source of strength when they recall how God has become real for them in that place.[7] In the last quarter century, more than religious groups have discovered the sacred quality that becomes attached to the places where their lives are shaped. Tony Hiss, for example, speaks for a mobile population in a changing world. He offers a contemporary lament as "development" and "progress" wipe out the foundations of memories that have sustained people over decades, sometimes over generations, and then he suggests reaffirmation, when even mundane locations take on sacred meaning.[8]

Younger generations of boomers and Xers are characterized by the experience of dislocation and discontinuity previously associated with immigrant groups. As a result, they gravitate toward a "journey theology,"[9] a desire to know and experience life while on the move. In response, small congregations need to identify and articulate the rooted values that nourish even those who see themselves constantly moving. Fortunately for small churches, several consulting authors have named the enduring values— values nurtured from their roots of memory and sunk deeply in the experience of intimate Christian communities.[10]

Further, small-church worship that hopes to reach younger and more mobile populations must be clear and intentional about the values they celebrate in corporate life of the church family, from the most formal act of worship to all its other actions in learning, work, and play. Since worship is the most public and intentional act, the symbolic objects and rituals in worship remain the most obvious expression of church beliefs and commitment. These are the moments that give meaning to the objects of our silent history.

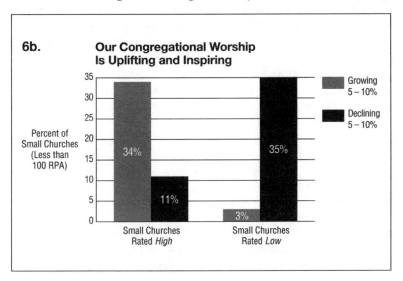

6b.

Our Congregational Worship Is Uplifting and Inspiring

Percent of Small Churches (Less than 100 RPA)

Uplifting worship has an unparalleled impact on congregational growth and vitality, according to FACT data (as seen in its positive relationship to growth and negative relationship to decline; see Fig. 6b). But to retain its appeal, worship must be relevant to the population the congregation is trying to reach (seen more dramatically in the FACT Report). In *Fifteen Services for Small Churches*, Elaine Strawn and Christine Nees lay out the calendar year of worship events designed intentionally for small congregations that want to draw others into their experiences while maintaining the core of their traditional meaning.[11] Like the elder who told me that "good worship is what I feel first and understand later," David Ray gives leaders of small congregations a solid workbook that mixes liturgy and ritual with images and practical themes that lay the foundations for worship that seems "powerful, naturally."[12]

To Make a Memorial

In one sense, all Christians have already shared in the silent history of our faith. Such a recognition of the past is embedded in the liturgy of communion. God has spoken to us in particular places through the love and words of particular people. The places and the people are embedded in our experience and carried with us through the rest of our lives. Raising these particulars up to conscious thanksgiving lies at the center of worship and provides the central theme for the liturgy of the Lord's Supper.

Max Thurian of the Taizé Community, in his study entitled *The Eucharist Memorial,* reminds us of the Hebraic roots for the final commandment of Jesus for the Eucharist: "Do this in remembrance *(anamnesis)* of me" (Luke 22:14-20; 1 Cor. 11:23-26). Thurian summarizes the liturgical actions expected when we "make a memorial" before the Lord: "To think of something known and past, a material something. . . . To recall man's sin and God covenant. . . . To recall something in favor of someone or against him. . . . To recall or remind God by means of sacrifice."[13]

Silent history is one way to make a memorial before the Lord. In our actions, we are thankful for the past, recognize our need for continued care, and restore the sense of using the gifts of God until we, like those who have gone before us, come home. To remember Christ, whether in the Lord's Supper or in meditation, is to feel his presence. To remember the church's history is to relive it and to learn from it. Large churches would do well to learn from small churches how to use their history to shape and energize the future of their ministries.

Some congregations have developed extensive healing ministries, and others have not. Those congregations who care only for themselves are becoming smaller and smaller. Eventually their place will have no meaning, for they have not shared it with anyone. They will have lost their remembrance. But those who serve others are saved from themselves. They have shared their place, and their history lives on in others. By definitions of ministry, a church is as large as the lives that are touched through its congregation, by the love of God. Caring is the ultimate measure of a congregation's size. In the eyes of God, some "small" churches are tremendous. God is remembered, and his remembrance is shared.

Suggestions for Further Reading

Gunderson, Gary. *Deeply Woven Roots: Improving the Quality of Life in Your Community*. Minneapolis: Fortress Press, 1997.
   Reattaching lost roots through past memories and current practices.

Kenneson, Philip D. *Life on the Vine: Cultivating the Fruit of the Spirit in Christian Community*. Downers Grove, Ill.: InterVarsity Press, 1999.
   Practical guide to values that transcend generational differences.

Pappas, Anthony G. *Mustard Seeds: Devotions for Small Church People*, available through Five Small Stones, 69 Weymouth Street, Providence, RI 02906.
   How sacred places and spirit-filled events sustain lives and change communities.

Ray, David R. *Wonderful Worship in Smaller Churches*, Cleveland: Pilgrim Press, 2000.
   Using small-church experience and commitments in memorable worship events.

A Calendar of
Annual Church Events

"Annual events" are those programs that the church sponsors annually for the whole membership, family, and friends of the church throughout the community. Some annual events require a heavy investment of the pastor's time and energy. Some are organized by church officers. Some are blessed by the official board but supported by the work of another group, such as the women's organization. Some annual events are barely tolerated by the officers and face annual opposition by the most recent pastor. They survive, like some couples, without benefit of clergy. Annual events often have the backing of "annual leaders" and the support of "annual members" for whom this event is the most significant activity in the church calendar. It is the reason they will claim to be church members when they sign in at the hospital, and perhaps even will remember it in their will.

The easiest procedure for developing the calendar of annual events is to list the months of the year, then write the events of each season next to the month when it usually happens. Even the smallest congregation can fill out a calendar of annual events. Frequently, smaller churches have more annual events for the whole congregation than meetings for separate groups with their individual interests. Churches that have relatively few organized weekly or monthly activities to list on their bulletin often generate an amazing informal network of planning and preparation for their own annual bash. By whatever name they may be called, every church has some annual events in the worship and the caring life of the congregation.

After recording each such event, note a few distinguishing differences: who will get the event organized? Some are official events that have the support of the church board, and others are so traditional that they would happen anyway. Who does the work? For pastors who say there is no leadership in their church, this moment is often revealing. Who attends? Who contributes? This is an indication of the historic relationship between church and community.

CHAPTER SEVEN

Events Worth Remembering

Identity for a small congregation is usually drawn from common experiences in the past (chapter 5) and focused in a particular place (chapter 6). Identity is maintained in the life of each congregation by the rhythm of events. Some events, like the choreography of worship, occur weekly. Other meetings are held monthly for the various groups of the congregation. These continuing experiences are their way of refreshing the relational glue that holds the social cell together. Beyond the rhythm of activity in the small church, community and national annual events provide the pulse for the life of the larger community.

Annual events offer an ingenious way for the relatively small caring cell of Christian faith to maintain an important role in the lives of many people who share a common history and a piece of turf. Annual events call people to be physically present to one another. These gatherings and celebrations reenact the source of their common values, and restate the basis of their common faith. A church will usually have several annual events throughout the year, to be enjoyed at such a pace that the resources of a few key people can be the catalyst for the release of much greater energy that otherwise would seem dormant or unavailable. Annual events provide good stewardship of people in the small congregation.

Annual events arouse many different feelings and satisfy many different kinds of needs. For the purpose of discussion, I have divided the events into four areas of satisfaction for the participants. In practice, no such formal distinctions are maintained.

- Annual events *mark the passage of time,* as the cycle of the seasons and as an affirmation of the caring community. Christmas and Easter are universally significant.
- Annual events *celebrate the moments of personal transition,* of change for the individual and renewed acceptance by the larger community. Graduation Sunday and birthday luncheons are examples.
- Annual events *recall the identity of the particular congregation* because of the experiences the members have shared and the people they care for. Homecomings and cemetery picnics are typical.
- Annual events *invite a wider segment of the community* to participate and to share in the ministry of the church to that community. The Harvest Bazaar and the Spring Pancake Supper are such events.

A word of caution: no small church has all these kinds of annual events. A single small congregation may host only half a dozen annual events and yet satisfy all four functions in each event. For purposes of discussion, I have used different examples to include more of the diversity of annual events now practiced in churches and to emphasize their different purposes. I hope to encourage each congregation in the development of a few annual events that are uniquely appropriate to the character and ministry of that congregation.

Passages of Time

Time passes. Annual events mark its passing with the affirmation of a faith that is bigger than we are, and a community of support that will outlast us. Time and space have been "staked out" in the annual event that recalls the past and reassures the believer about the continuity of God's care and community support into the unfolding unknown. In a classic study, Lloyd Warner notes this use of the annual event:

Time . . . is a yearly cycle which tidily begins, contains, and completes a unit of duration. Each yearly cycle is related at its two ends. . . . Often a festival marks the point where one link ends and a new one begins, thus ritualizing the separation of the past

from the future time. . . . Enclosed within this system, collective
memories of yesterday become a reliable and dependable map
for knowing what will happen tomorrow, thus reducing anxiety
about the future's uncertainties.[1]

Christmas-New Year (the winter solstice) is the seasonal transition most universally celebrated. One of the events in the
Christmas octave usually has the largest attendance in the year.
For once, everybody comes. The music reflects the binding of past
and present: the strength of the old and the brightness of the new.
This is one time (event) when the congregation sings its loudest
and best. This is often the event when the children enact the faith
and so incorporate the meaning of belonging far below the levels
of consciousness. The children's pageant, candlelight, carols, and
communion are mixed with Sunday school class parties and the
trimming of the Christmas tree "the way we always did it."

The formal worship is authorized by the board and clearly
managed by the pastor or leading members. But the momentum
of the event is much larger than any individual or small official
group. Christmas is the annual event that will happen according
to unwritten tradition.

Christmas-New Year is not the only periodic celebration that
marks the passage of time. Westerhoff and Neville have observed
that "summer" in the United States has become a form of sacred
time based on the institutional shift of public schools, a pattern
also established in response to the agricultural economic base in
which children were needed as field hands during growing season and harvest time. Now we have two ritually celebrated all-
American holidays to mark this shift—Memorial Day to begin
and Labor Day to close."[2]

Many congregations have tried to institutionalize annual events
that would parallel the "sacred time" of the larger society. They
have altered the hour of worship in the summer, combined with
other congregations for worship, and joined in ecumenical gatherings to acknowledge a faith that is bigger than each congregation.
At the same time, they have tried to mark off the summer season,
with a transitional event in the spring and an annual rally in the fall.

Some churches have been successful in developing these
rhythms. Most have pushed hard and produced little. Anthro-
pologist Gwen Kennedy Neville explains: "In American society

we can observe at least three concurrent calendar "years" in progress—that of the school, the church, and the commercial-industrial complex. Each will have its own cycles and rhythms. Each will have activity shifts marked by rituals restating periodically its own group position, beliefs, values, and world view."[3]

There is a fourth calendar that must be observed: sports schedules and seasons mark out important events in the rhythm of the year. Along with the other calendars, we also have high-school sports and Monday night football, local community events, and the opening day for hunting and fishing. Sensitive church leaders not only avoid conflicts between calendars but, more important, they use transitional events to celebrate the seasons and integrate our different times into an experience of the whole year

At the deepest level, annual events do more than block out time—they offer purpose to the group and meaning to its members. Thus Warner writes: "The yearly story of the life of Christ expresses and evokes some of the deepest and most significant emotions men [and women] feel about themselves and the world in which they live. The great drama necessarily releases them from quandaries and dilemmas for which rational and moral values have no answers."[4]

Easter, the celebration of the Resurrection, is the annual event that provides the keystone in the arch of Christian time. Faced with the puzzling fact of personal death, the community affirms its faith in the transcendence of God and the eternal life of the believer. Easter provides what John Westerhoff calls the "primary means of intentional religious socialization, . . . [and gives] opportunities for the community . . . to experience and reflect upon its faith and thereby evolve an integrated set of answers to questions about oneself and the world."[5] The season of Lent—culminating in the darkness of Maundy Thursday, the stillness of Good Friday, the dawn of Easter Sunday—recalls many events that have been widely used as moments for the most significant annual event for the members of small churches.[6] The time speaks truth to eternal questions.

Personal Transitions

Annual events often reflect and speak to the personal journey of members in the church. Gwen Kennedy Neville writes: "The ceremonies surrounding the life cycle of individuals are found at those times when the person is in transition from one biological or social state to another. At birth, puberty, marriage, parenthood, menopause, and death the individual is passing through changes that will effect her or his interaction with other group members."[7]

Transitional moments are reflected in regularly scheduled annual events. Graduation is a time of passage for the child and youth; commencement marks an end and a beginning. Graduation Sunday may reflect the transitional moment, but often the young people have institutionalized their own annual event to celebrate their passage. Annual trips to the beach and graduation parties without restricting hours are annual events that church officers do not plan, but widely accept, condone, and remember. Birthday luncheons by the women's organization, memorial flowers on a particular Sunday, and lilies at Easter may all mark similar adjustments to the personal transitions that have found a place in the regular life of the congregation.

Most moments of personal transition arrive unannounced and cannot be scheduled on the calendar, but they are among the most significant annual events for the congregation. In faith, the congregation is prepared for these events. They have been anticipated but unscheduled. The life of Jesus reflects "the marks of his own rites of passage, conforming in broad outline to Van Gennep's classical conception of what they are in all societies. They include birth, naming, circumcision, the miraculous events that mark his maturity, the Crucifixion, Resurrection, Ascension."[8] When the time comes for these passages, all other time stops. The larger, extended family will gather from distant parts of the country and will linger enough to get caught up with one another. They will share in the solemn celebration of death, the joy of marriage, anguish of illness, or the cries of new life.

Times of personal transition become instant annual events for that year. They are not exceptions. They are expected in the life of faith, but simply are not on the calendar. Personal transition events should be added to your list of annual events and anticipated in every congregation. They provide three essential functions: first, events of personal transition bring together and identify family ties within the larger community. They offer the first contact for an amazing number of eligible marriage partners, who first met as "a friend of the family."[9] Second, these events bring the family face-to-face with the deepest questions about transition: death, life, family, and the world beyond. These events are interpreted not only with words, but also by the presence of the larger caring cell.[10] Third, these unscheduled annual events provide contacts with people most likely to respond to the invitation for church membership. They are already self-identified "friends of the family."

Congregational Identity

"I didn't really understand what was happening," the young pastor explained. "In my first year I was advised that 'we've started making plans for the annual homecoming. Is that all right?' Before I could answer—no reply was expected—the elder continued, 'Mr. Walton takes care of the place that night, and his daughter arranges the food,' and so on. I didn't say anything then, and I haven't been asked since. But it is a great occasion, and one of the biggest attendance events of the year. It would be the largest worship if they all came to church, but they don't. The crowd comes after worship, for the social!"

The pastor was describing the most familiar and informal sort of annual event. It can be called the Harvest Dinner or Ladies' Night at the Men's Club or the Men's Dinner at Christmas or the Summer Picnic. Whatever the designation, the result is the same. This is *the* time when everyone knows that everyone else will be there.

Plentiful food,[11] ample time, and old friends are the marks of most annual homecomings. The timing and focus of homecoming events may have powerful symbolic meaning, or, in my view, it may be an historical accident. Some get attached to the Christmas tree trimming, and others to the rolling of Easter eggs. We could find no consistency to the choice of homecoming themes, except that it was the church's own. The uniqueness of the event is matched only by the autonomous character of its leadership. Some leaders are officers of the congregation, and others will not be seen from one year to the next. Some have charts and lists, and others just let it all fall into place. Generally, the pastor is not needed to organize or even intrude upon the "planning." One pastor even said, "If I didn't come, they would never miss me." Clearly, the event is given by and for the members of the church. In fact, in one congregation, the members joked that an annual event was "what the 'past pastor' was opposed to, which is why he's the last 'past pastor.' "

So important is the annual event that it has been permitted into the liturgy of many congregations. In a similar context, Warner notes: "Perhaps one of the most significant changes in the contemporary Protestant church has been the recent introduction of several special family days into their sacred calendar—all of them coming from the influence of the laity on the church."[12] Mother's Day has become a time of reunion and renewal in many congregations, combining the affirmations of the extended family and of the intimate church. Other congregations designate a Founder's Day, sometimes even a homecoming weekend. One pastor described it as "well-organized disorder, from the opening prayer to the last piece of chicken." He said, "It lasts all day, but keeps the congregation in an uproar for a month of preparation."

Homecoming events provide a basic beat to the program of the small congregation. Larger churches can keep many activities and events moving at the same time. The energy of the small church must pulsate. In the annual homecoming, a relatively few people can release the energy of many more people who have shared the place and the love of the congregation. As Christmas-New Year is to the calendar and Easter is to the whole church, so the annual homecoming is a time of unique and personal renewal in the life of the small church. Again, Gwen Kennedy Neville: "A scattered-and-gathered community is especially useful in a highly mobile society such as ours as a means of identifying the community of cultural significance."[13]

Identity is often established by the affirmation of a common past. One rural homecoming is called the Cemetery Picnic. It is not a morbid or maudlin event to remember the virtues of ancestors who are buried in the church cemetery. The Cemetery Picnic has utilitarian value by generating the imperative to clean the cemetery and "show our respect for the dead." The picnic, or feast, of many special dishes, is not literally *in* the cemetery, but is held *on the grounds* of the church. And it may take the whole weekend!

A more lively urban affirmation of ancestry is found in the ethnic congregations that recall the culture of the old country. One Hungarian Reformed congregation will spend months in planning for the annual Festival of the Grapes. Women begin weeks in advance to prepare the traditional Hungarian foods. To confound the Reformed tradition in America, one observer reports, "There is dancing in the church basement, and the food is accompanied by quantities of wine, beer, and hard liquor, sometimes in staggering amounts."

After visiting many homecoming events in small congregations, and larger churches as well, I believe that this kind of annual event provides a useful index for the future of the church. Some congregations have relatively large numbers of people to return, but I believe that these congregations will die. Some may not have as many, but they will be sustained and might even grow. The difference is not in the numbers of people who return, but in the way that some congregations expand the event to include the new members in their preparations. The event is significant in the identity of the congregation. The new member who has helped in the annual event is really adopted into the family. He has shared the preparation for the family "birthday party" of the congregation.

In a similar way, congregations that invite the community to share in its annual celebration will be twice blessed: the community will be stronger for the presence of the church, and the church will be stronger through its public affirmation. Unfortunately, many such annual homecomings are escapes from the present, with the same old people doing the same old things and complaining about the same old problems. They are, as one member observed, "like having tea in the morgue."

Expanding Ministries

By contrast, some small congregations have found that their most effective annual events reach out and embrace others in their community. In one church, it happened this way: what was once the Men's Club fish fry to benefit the youth program of the church was expanded. The Men's Club is defunct, but the whole community joins with the church to raise the funding for the summer program, which the church sponsors for the children of the area.

Another church started an annual Valentine party for older people who lived in a retirement home nearby. The party for the elderly has become so popular that it goes on long after the elderly return to the home. It has become an annual event for the congregation, as well as a high point in the calendar of the retirement home.

Watermelon cuttings in the country and rummage sales in the city (and vice versa) have often been a way of mingling church members and neighbors, providing both with the common cause of developing resources for improving the community. Most of these annual events are hidden under the rubric of "fund-raisers." They may raise money, but they accomplish much more. One women's group leader reports that the annual fair is the only event "where most all of the members contribute something. All of the work is done by the women of the church, of course, with a little help from a few men. The pastors don't even know what's happening."

Sometimes the church leaders get involved in ways that reverse the roles of leadership and make the church more like a family. One teenager says she likes best to work on the annual bazaar because "we are one family then. I have even seen the pastor cooking and the clerk of the council washing dishes." Healthy churches have developed an identity from annual events that seek to serve in the community. All annual events will not be directed to reach nonmembers. But no church can escape its own self-centered concerns without some organized effort to reach out.

Hidden Curriculum

Even the church building takes on the meaning of the events that occur there, a significance that is not missed by either the younger members or the families in the neighborhood. John Westerhoff writes:

> The church building itself, set in the community, is a "school-house." It reveals its people to themselves, tells them about their beliefs, attitudes, and values. . . . The church is a classroom without walls, offering for people of all ages—especially the impressionable young—a boundless hidden curriculum."[14]

"Christian education is more than Sunday church school," explain two pastors who have been there.[15] The Sunday church school in many congregations provides the most important link in the chain of regular events. For some, the church school is even more important than the more formal worship experience. The organizational structure may be elaborate enough to provide a place for everyone (although it may function without regard to who holds which position). The rhythm of the Sunday school may be far more important than the content of the courses. As one forlorn pastor said: "I had to discover that the Sunday school was doing more important things than providing education. It was 'communication central' for the life of our church." The church rescheduled the more formal educational activities so that they would not compete with the caring rhythm of the Sunday school.[16] That level of commitment is reflected in the FACT data, showing that traditional Sunday school, youth, and community service are the highest priority for small churches (Fig. 7). Notice the very high commitment that larger churches invest in youth programs, but smaller churches generally spend a larger part of their budget simply to do as well as they can. As for the importance of the choir, as one pianist explained, "In our small church, everyone is considered a member of the choir."

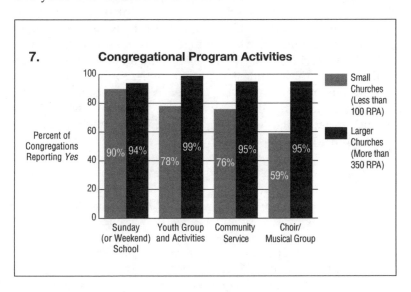

7.   Congregational Program Activities

"Just because God makes everything fresh doesn't mean that he throws out the old," explained one church member following a meditation on Revelation 21:5. The rhythm of expected events holds together the people of the small church. The annual events and human transitions provide the high points in the rhythm of events. But the backbone of the caring cell is found in the flow of activities. Weekly and monthly routine happenings hold the core of the congregation together. Like the human body, the small congregation finds its strength in carefully ordered habits that do not require continued examination and do not anticipate radical changes.

The identity of the congregation is reconfirmed in the rhythms of worship. The most militant hymns are metered and transposed into a key that fits the congregation. The most challenging sermons are absorbed into a network of caring people whose identity is found in continuing what they have done before. Change is possible and coping is essential, as we will see in the subsequent chapters. But the reassuring rhythm of the congregation keeps them going.

Regular meetings are part of the pace for the small congregation. The meetings may be called for a variety of purposes, but the regularity of participation provides the basic satisfaction for the membership. Meetings are a way of keeping in touch with those who are present and keeping up with those who are not there. The meetings may be called for Bible study or fund-raising, but people-time remains the dominant item of discussion. Sunday school and youth ministries are highest on the small-church priorities for meetings.[17] Often these meetings are focused on the children and youth, while many others in the congregation gather nearby. One mother observed, "When it's a youth program, the kids are inside and the adults on the steps, and when it's a women's gathering, we're on the inside and they're on the steps—but we are always mostly all here."

Pastoral calling is another part of the regular identity of the congregation. Some evidence of the pastor's presence personally in the homes of members, or publicly in the mainstream of the community, is often mentioned as a part of the essential satisfactions of belonging in a small congregation. Some pastors cannot separate rhythm from routine. "I am fed up with routine," said one pastor. "When the habits get engrained, what's the difference between coming to church and catching the bus to work? It's all routine." Yet these rhythms of church participation should offer more. They are not simply habits of order and process. These events provide, on a regular basis, what is available in more dramatic form at the annual events: an opportunity for renewal through contact with the transcendent. As Mircea Eliade says, "The experience of sacred space . . . not only project[s] a fixed point into the formless fluidity of profane space . . . it also effects a break in the plane, that is, it opens communication between cosmic planes (between earth and heaven)."[18] Thus the importance of the Sabbath, the sacred time in a sacred place, as symbolic of the conversation between this world and the next.

Turf Stewardship

The pulse of regular events in the small congregation provides an appropriate context for brief reflections on raising funds—it's a natural part of congregational rhythm. In the caring cell, money is like time: it is not evenly distributed. As one treasurer explained: "We have two kinds of money problems, the regular and the emergencies. The emergencies are easy. It's the regular bills that kill us." Small congregations have unique problems with systems for budget planning and financial management. The caring cell does not respond well to every-member canvass, every-member pledging, and year-round budgeting.

The every-member canvass is a problem for the caring cell. It presumes that members know one another, but not too well. The callers should know the family called on by name, but they should not be socially or economically dependent upon them. Of course, in the caring cell, people know one another too well. They must depend upon one another too much. They are too close to press the questions that must be asked, and they know too much to use the pre-printed literature. The whole process feels "canned."

Pledging is also a problem for many caring cells. Pledging assumes that the church members plan what they do with both their time and their money. Pledging is part of budgeting. That is a problem in rural areas, in urban areas, and among the elderly everywhere. Rural communities are often still in economic harmony with the seasons: "What we do not have (yet), we cannot give." Urban minorities are faced with an economic instability that does not know the limitations of the seasons. Older people often live on marginal incomes with the constant threat of financial crises. Pledging is not a natural form of giving for those whose future is so beset with uncertainties.

Budget planning in the small church is often "intuitive," based on the expertise of a treasurer who has practiced for a generation. There is no printed budget and no monthly statements that compare this year with former "year to date" reports. The officers are expected to know these things, and the membership is expected to trust them.

In the small church, the right people "know." They know what people have given, what they will give, and what they are capable of giving. They know what are the church debts and what are the anticipated expenses. They "know," much as the family store is run from the cashbox and the checking account. In turn, the members know how much they are expected to give. Most small congregations give with amazing accuracy and consistency.

Church finance is not a system of pledging or budgeting. It is a "family process" of expecting and receiving. One pastor says: "In the ten years I have been here, the pledges have never equaled the budget. But the current receipts have more than equaled our needs, at the last minute." Another pastor explains: "The small church can receive a better-than-average response from its people, because they have a strong sense of loyalty. They know their contribution is important."

Actually, it is not accurate to say that small-church members give more than members of larger congregations. In some churches they do, in some they do not. The difference is simply this: when the need is perceived, the small church will stretch to meet it. The small church will stretch to build or remodel their place, the building. The small church will stretch to have the services of a pastor, shared or full-time. The small church will stretch to help people in need. But the members will not give blindly to the church budget. Further, they will not accept a goal that they feel is personally unreachable. In most caring cells, they give what they have been giving, minus just a little "to make sure that I am still needed."

One pastor summarized the dilemma: "We just can't face an every-member canvass. But we have developed a concept of stewardship in response to need, real people need. That's what works." Healthy congregations know the kind of service that their money provides. "When I first came into the ministry," one pastor recalls, "I would have given the widow back her mite. I would have said, 'It's all right, keep it.' I had to learn to let the congregation care about people as much as I did." Once the congregation discovers the satisfactions of caring, "the money can be raised by a phone call."

In turf stewardship, the caring-cell church will take care of its own. Within the lifestyle of the small congregation, membership giving has increased substantially when the congregation has

seen the real need, when they have designed the program themselves, and when they have kept the process very personal. One
fund-raiser consultant explains a stewardship program that fits
these criteria, and it can be homegrown in any congregation. He
begins with the assumption that people know a great deal about
one another in the caring-cell church, that they see a need in the
ministry of the church, and that they are looking for a way to help
the congregation meet that need on an increased, financially sustaining basis. Under these conditions, the leaders of several congregations have responded favorably and continuously to a
program of "step-up stewardship."

Step-up stewardship expects the officers to divide the congregation according to levels of giving: $5 per week, $10 per week,
$25 per week, $40 per week, and so on. The number of families at
each level is counted (but not the names are not revealed). To
achieve the goal that has been commonly agreed upon, each person (or family) is asked to take one step up to the next level. This
is not a pledge and not a percentage-of-income approach. In the
caring cell, it is a request that members think of themselves as
"one step higher than you were." Within the values of the caring-
cell church, it works to help the congregation accomplish what
they feel needs to be done.

Another means of raising funds is through the annual events.
Although this is only a minor portion of the total church budget,
annual events can be significant in the total financial needs of the
congregation. Further, annual events can confirm the adoption of
new members into the church family, and it can attract outsiders
into the flow of congregational life.

At the base, when the need is associated with one of their own,
the urgency of giving is transformed. Not self-denial and discipline, but satisfaction and pride can dominate the stewardship of
the caring cell. Giving can be "fun" when they know how it helps
the place that they shared and the life that they live here
together—and beyond.

A Healthy Church

The health of a congregation is difficult to measure, especially
when we are more concerned with quality than quantity, with

spiritual than with material characteristics. Yet I believe that there are signs of health that we must take seriously:

- A healthy church will care about the members of that congregation, and respond to their needs.
- A healthy church will care about the turf, the place, and the larger community where God has called it to be. In the act of healing, a healthy church will share its place with those in need.
- A healthy church will have an identity that is carried in the rhythm and pace of the congregation's life together. The identity they share comes from God, who touches them as a people in a place.

Small churches are sick when their members lose the touch of caring for one another, healing in the community, and pacing the power that comes from God. In all these ways, a small church must seek to be healthy. But sometimes health is a blessing that comes when a congregation makes a commitment to be an effective instrument of healing for others.

Suggestions for Further Reading

Chandler, Russell. *Feeding the Flock: Restaurants and Churches You'd Stand in Line For.* Bethesda, Md.: Alban Institute, 1998.
  Through restaurant images, congregations appear fresh and appetizing.

Foltz, Nancy T. *Caring for the Small Church: Insights from Women in Ministry.* Valley Forge, Pa.: Judson Press, 1994.
  How ritual can sustain formative experiences.

Klassen, Ron and John Koessler. *No Little Places.* Grand Rapids: Baker Books, 1996.
  Education is a lifestyle in the mutuality of small churches in small towns.

Nancy T. Foltz, ed. *Religious Education in the Small Church.* Birmingham, Ala.: Religious Education Press, 1990.
  Essays by seasoned practitioners.

PART THREE

Sharing

"Your stuff is poison," one urban pastor told me. "It's only good to appease the gray heads of old churches, and to incite the hotheads of ghetto churches. You tempt a church to wallow in the past and make the pastor like it. Your approach may ease the pain of dying churches, but you have not shown us how to help the church to live!"

The pastor was wrong, in part. Caring and belonging are neglected elements of health in many small churches. These virtues should be put out front, to be admired and continued. Human relationships and conserving the faith provide the unique dynamics that distinguishes many small congregations. They are Christian virtues that should not play second fiddle to other alternatives.

The pastor is also correct. If we spoke only of caring and belonging, we would be inadequate to the Christian faith, and incomplete in describing the small church. We would have emphasized the past and the personal, but slighted the importance of sharing in the present. Faith must move past experience to share in the present and to anticipate the future. To shape a changing world, the small church uses its experience of caring and its style of belonging as its foundation for sharing. Sharing suggests dealing effectively with the difficult, the unexpected, and the mundane. Sharing has a quality of stability, if not success. It does not conquer and vanquish the world, but rather endures and lives in harmony.

Small churches' sharing is expressed in three ways, which will be considered in the following chapters:

- Effective small churches have a clarity of purpose that fits with their identity, in the midst of which they can accommodate great conflict.
- Resolute small churches are comfortable with the kind of quiet witness they make in their community and beyond.
- Affirming small churches declare that they are members in the Body of Christ by sharing with others across faith differences.

Church Groups, Goals, and Purposes

This exercise in matching can be most effective when it is attempted individually first, and then the results are shared with the whole group by constructing a composite picture together.

Draw a line down the center of a working sheet of paper (several sheets may be required, marked the same way). On the left side, make a list of the purposes and goals of the church. Begin with the most formal statements, such as a biblical covenant, liturgical creed, or the preamble of the church by-laws, if these are available and appropriate. Next, list the formal goals that the official church boards may have accepted as targets for the current calendar year or for long-range programs. Finally, list your own informal statements of purpose. Many small churches will list only the informal purposes. These should include the satisfaction and services that the church provides for individuals, families, and the larger community.

On the right side of the paper, list the organizations and activities of the church. Begin with the most formal and official boards. Include all the Sunday school classes, fellowship groups, service clubs, and prayer circles. Note especially the larger and inclusive activities such as Sunday worship, family-night suppers, and annual events. Last, list the most informal groups, such as the sofa-sitters in the coffee hours, or the men who always have Sunday school class in the kitchen, or the families who share doughnuts and coffee every Sunday after worship.

Finally, match the two sides. Show the relationship between the goals and purposes on the left, and the church organizations and activities on the right. This can be indicated by using numbers for each of the goals and purposes on the left side, and letters for each group or activity on the right and then matching numbers with letters. Or it can be done by a carefree connection of lines drawn from each item on the left to the appropriate activity on the right.

CHAPTER EIGHT

Goals, Conflicts, and Renewal

Goals for the church are important mainly for the clarity that they provide. Goal statements make specific what purpose statements leave vague and general. Goals provide clarity of purpose, a sense of progress, and a measurable standard for evaluation. They offer guidelines for the allocation of resources and a standard of accountability for the organizational groups that make up the life of the church. Goal statements are especially helpful in the management of the church and especially satisfying to those who feel the need for more clarity of general purposes.

Most small churches lack that kind of clarity in their statements of church goals. Yet they have deep commitments to the purposes of the church. Smaller congregations distinguished themselves by the quiet character of their faith, the importance of Christian fellowship, and the urgency for the church to respond to people in need, while, as we have noted, churches with larger congregations emphasize clear vision, program diversity, and process efficiency.

Small churches have strong, but often implicit, commitments. Some may have a statement of purpose in the liturgy. Many more find their purpose embedded in the things that they are doing, have been doing, and expect to continue doing: Sunday worship, Sunday school, pastoral care, response to personal crises, maintenance of building (and cemetery), family events, prayer and study groups, women's organizations, the rhythm of official boards and informal groups. In a general way, they want to spread the gospel, preserve community standards, bind families together, and be of use in the community and of service to the

Lord. More than one has considered "training seminary students" as part of their purpose. These are the commitments they already have, even if they never appear on a statement of goals.

One pastor complained, "I can't get them to talk about goals or examine what they are doing. But they don't stop, they just keep doing." One expert in industrial management process volunteered to help the representatives of a small congregation develop a clear statement of goals. When the retreat was over, he shook his head in disbelief and frustration. Under his pressure, they had written a statement, but he doubted if it would ever be used. "They appear to be goalless and drifting," he said, "and yet they are determined to survive, too stubborn to change, and quick to respond to a person in need. They may not have goals, but they surely have deep commitments."[1]

A look at the exercise "Church Groups, Goals, and Purposes" should be instructive. First, for individuals it will suggest those programs about which each person has the greatest interest— usually positive, but sometimes negative. The groups we support tend to be fulfilling more of our purposes, and those we doubt tend to be associated with marginal purposes, from our perspective. We discover that we need each other to be able to see the whole.

Second, official boards and committees (or task forces) tend to be associated with specific goals. Informal purposes seem more appropriately associated with informal groups. In general, the small church will have fewer goals as such, but several strong commitments to general purposes for groups in the congregation.

Third, goal statements are more important to groups with new members. Goal statements provide an introduction and orientation for newcomers who have not shared the experiences and crises well known to many older members of the congregation. Newcomers, including the pastor, often find goal statements very helpful.

Fourth, it should be clear that the caring cell can embrace a number of activities without losing touch with its members. Usually members are surprised at how much is really going on, especially in the areas of informal gatherings of people who mutually care for and support one another.

Commitment to purpose can sustain the small church over long periods of time. Goals are more appropriate if the church seeks to measure change and to feel a sense of accomplishment. Purposes serve maintenance functions; goals serve management functions. The purpose of a congregation is "to praise God," while the goal may be stated as "to increase the number who attend worship by 10 percent." When compared to larger, more organized churches, the small church typically has stated fewer goals. Its priority is people, and progress is a by-product. Its purpose is appropriate to the kind of group that many small churches feel themselves to be. Technically, they can be said to be "goalless." But that should never be confused with the absence of determined purposefulness. To confuse the absence of goals with the absence of purpose is like suggesting that those who do not speak English do not know how to talk.

Members of small churches are often personally familiar with goal-setting procedures. Most have participated in some sort of goal setting in their places of employment, and many congregations have engaged in redevelopment programs based on clarity of purpose and measurable goals. Greater clarity of goals is particularly helpful: (1) when the leadership is new or new leadership is desirable (as in the entry process for pastors); (2) when the resources (usually money) are limited, and the board must make difficult decisions; (3) when a change is desirable in the informal character of the congregation; or (4) when growth is possible in the size of church membership.

Three problems result from the implementation of goal setting in the small congregation:

- First, some members find difficulty in articulating the faith-ties that make the church worth attending, and goal setting appears to print what has remained unspoken.
- Second, the process elicits a new dimension of skills and relationships among the present leadership, which may produce another layer of church leadership. At a rather primitive level, we can see three kinds of lay leaders that are important to the process.
- Third, goal setting can precipitate conflict, which leaders must learn how to use constructively.

These are natural conditions within the caring cell, but they are rarely considered in most goal-setting discussions. To the rational planner, these responses may prove awkward, unexpected, and even destructive. In the end, I will argue in favor of clarifying goals—when it is done in ways consistent with small-church ethos.

Printing the Unspeakable

"I tried to get the board to set down our goals," said the pastor, "but they just would not get specific." In another church, a woman elder just sat there with her arms crossed. "It's really sacrilegious to put measurements on the power and love of God," she said. With a deep sadness, she continued, "I really don't feel right about this program." In another congregation, the elder-teacher of a Sunday school class called the program "manipulation of feelings," and stated that the purposes of the church are "the same yesterday, today, and forever." For many small churches, goal setting is, as one old-timer explained, "like stating the obvious, like trying to explain a joke."

People who resist participation in the total process often fail to find the words for their disapproval. When they describe their reluctance, it usually falls somewhere among these six reasons:

(1) Some people do not like voting that divides the congregation. They do not mind voting when it affirms what they are doing together or supports a report of some dimension in the life of the church. But they do not like to divide the house when forced to choose one of several people for one office or to choose priorities among different church programs. They want to affirm the group, not divide the church family. One person wanted to know if we voted in making family decisions at home: "Do the kids vote with the parents, or do you wait until you know what is best to do as a family?" These members were more comfortable when given the choice among affirmatives or when told "only the positive votes will count." Or perhaps more like a family, give the information to the trusted leaders and let them work it out.

(2) Some members resist putting the purposes and goals of the church in anything other than biblical phrases or general statements. One person announced: "The real reasons I attend cannot

be put into words, and I believe that is true for everyone. To write anything less than the truth is irrelevant." She was more comfortable when the leader distinguished between the "purposes of the church" (for which she attended) and the "goals" of particular church activities.

(3) Some people resist systems, processes, procedures, committees, reports, resource allocation, and all management techniques. One urban ethnic member observed that it reminded him too much of the place where he worked, "with time clocks to punch in and work sheets to fill out." He recommended that the church should live on "people-time, which begins when we get here and lasts as long as we can remember." He did not like what he called a "creeping system." Only the informality of the group would bring him along.

(4) Some object to the way the goal-setting process emphasizes the future. "Goal statements tend to emphasize what we will do, and neglect what we are doing," observed one pastor. A layman protested, "We can't always plow up the present for the sake of the future, not every year." One old-timer objected that "goals are the game of the pastor, and he doesn't even know us yet." These people are more at ease when they can see that the goals are an expression of the more permanent purposes of the church.

(5) Some feel that the goal statements are too subjective and self-serving. Unless questions are carefully phrased, they suggest that we are submitting God to a referendum. "God is not up for election," said one vigorous young Christian. "The question is not, 'What do I want?' Or even, 'What do we all want?' The question must be, 'What does God want of my life and of our lives together?'" He suggested that even the purpose of the church must be subject to constant review in the light of the revealed Word. For this concern, goal setting may be accompanied by study of key Scripture.

(6) Last, there are people who feel that goal setting is a betrayal of the most basic relationship between people and pastor. In their view, the pastor who knows and loves his people will lead them right. He or she should not need to ask the congregation or the board to set the goals or the priorities of the church. The pastor should "know." As one grandmother explained: "I know what my family needs before they ask. God knows my needs even before I am conscious of that need. If you really knew and loved

us, Pastor, you would not have to ask for a vote of the congregation. You should *know*." The comment seems to originate from the same sort of person who would expect the pastor to visit her in the hospital even if nobody passed the word that she was there. In both cases, she seems to be saying, "But you're my pastor, *you* should *know*."

In all of these concerns, the small-church pastor can confirm that they come with their own convictions, but pray to be enriched by views of the members and empowered by the continuing presence of the Holy Spirit.

Three Sorts of Leaders

Relational congregations have a "people first" style of making decisions. When the committees meet, the members spend much of the time getting caught up on the lives of other committee members, and members of their families, and members of their families' families. I remember a discussion that began with the need to fix the church roof. It went like this: "Mr. Smith was the last person to get up on the roof and fix it." "You know his daughter moved to California, and left the old man alone." "I heard that his daughter is sick out there." "No, I believe it's her baby that's sick." "Baby's in the hospital out there, the way I heard it." The original item was the need to fix the roof. It provided a chance for several people to catch up on the Smith family. At many such meetings, most of the time is spent catching up on people. In the final five minutes, they decide about the program—as one pastor playfully says, "To do it again like we did it before—whatever 'it' was."

For some people, planning, goal setting, and achieving change are emotionally satisfying, but not for everyone. Programs of congregational development bring the spirit of order and intentionally into the official board meetings. The change is more than procedural. It changes the climate of the group and the satisfactions of its membership. Good management procedure brings out a different side of the existing leaders, or it may attract different leaders altogether. As one delighted pastor explained, "Goal setting brings out the best *in* our leaders, and the best *of* our leaders." Unfortunately, as we have seen, some members get lost in the shuffle.

I find three sorts of leadership styles among the leaders in small churches. More than a century ago, Max Weber suggested that leadership could be characterized as traditional, rational, and charismatic.[2] Some contemporary church consultants with wide experience discover similar distinctions: "An underlying assumption of our model is that church leadership is required to fulfill three basic tasks. . . . (1) Associational [traditional] leadership provides effective guidance for gathering membership . . . with a free commitment to the mission of the church. (2) Organizational [rational] leadership (provides) . . . careful, efficient administration. (3) Spiritual [charismatic] leadership . . . helps people know themselves through the eyes of faith."[3]

Personally I think the *organizers* (rational leaders) are the easiest to find—often they find you first, with an agenda in one hand and a calendar in the other. They are the managers of church events, the "first sergeants" of the congregation, the chief chefs among the "sisters of the skillet" in the kitchen. They look like the people in charge, and others seem happy to let them do it. But two other sorts of leaders are at least as powerful. The *socializers* (traditional leaders) are embedded in the group, and they provide the social glue to hold the church together. They are the storytellers, entertainers, and gossips (wise and otherwise). They are the community "mothers" and sometimes the grumblers. Since they keep the group well knit together, the organizers are well advised not to alienate the socializers. The third sort of leaders I call the *saints* (charismatic leaders), who have a very special role in small church decision-making. They are the venerated confidants and caregivers who have soaked up the church into their person, and whom the church trusts most when a major decision is at hand. More than simply senior status, these members symbolize what it means to belong. As one awed pastor told me, "When it comes to a big decision, all the others can talk on and on, but when the saint has nodded, the talkin's over."

Of course, like a drama with a small cast, some people play more than one role and the allocation of roles can change over time. In most small churches, all three roles contribute to the decisions, but on an organizational chart you are less likely to find the names of socializers or saints recognized as official leaders. At times, the pastor may be pressured to play one or another role, sometimes as organizer, other times to provide the pastoral social glue. Theologian Urban Holmes names the primary role of clergy as *"theotokas,* one who 'bears God' to humankind," the symbol of the holy in the religious community.[4] Holmes's description of *theotokas* does not limit the clergy to a charismatic role, but embraces all three leadership tasks—relational, organizational, and charismatic, and that combination is too heavy for many clergy. Whatever their personal role, pastors should at least be sensitive to the variety of characters in the congregation and to the various roles they contribute to reaching congregational decisions.

Conflict over Goals

Goal setting sometimes precipitates conflict. Despite a variety of books and other resources available in workshops, articles, and through consultants, the problem of conflict surfaces in every discussion of congregational development in the small church. "How can we deal with conflict," asks one pastor, "when it always seems to break out over very small matters?" Another pastor, well into the goal-setting process, complained, "Our congregation can handle the big issues, but we break up over the personal issues and petty arguments." It seems as if fighting is a way of life in the small church.

Conflict is natural and even necessary, according to the classic study of Lewis Coser. He says: "Conflict is a form of socialization. . . . Groups require disharmony as well as harmony, dissociation as well as association; and conflicts within them are by no means altogether disruptive factors."[5]

Small congregations prove particularly susceptible to social conflict. Members of a caring cell have relationships that are not personally threatened by the transitory fighting over petty concerns. The pastor who looks for an organizational solution does not appreciate the nature of the conflict. Thus, one rural pastor writes: "I keep hoping to find an organizational way to deal with conflict. We have a congregation of several large families, and the feuds are built in. Most of our conflict is petty and personal." That situation is, in Coser's view, a stable relationship:

Stable relationships may be characterized by conflicting behavior. Closeness gives rise to frequent occasions for conflict, but if the participants feel that their relationships are tenuous, they will avoid conflict, fearing that it might endanger the continuance of the relation. When close relationships are characterized by frequent conflicts rather than by the accumulation of hostile and ambivalent feelings, we may be justified, given that such conflicts are not likely to concern basic consensus, in taking these frequent conflicts as an index of the stability of these relationships.[6]

In other words, in a stable, healthy, trusting small congregation, members will not manage the conflict: they are free to fight. Further, Coser adds, in close proximity, the conflict may be more intense. Thus, they may not fight more often; but when they do, it's a lulu. They are free to fight, because they are held together by bonds that are deeper than reasons or issues. As FACT data confirms, smaller congregations are more likely to report "serious conflict" in the past five years, and rate themselves lower than larger congregations in dealing with conflict openly. (Fig. 8a)

Professional sensitivity to the appropriate pastoral response to conflict is a question of too much complexity to be considered in this context. In his book *In the Cross Fire,* Donald P. Smith has gathered a wealth of relevant materials. James Allen Sparks has processed in his book *Potshots at the Preacher* many of the relevant questions in a most usable form. In general, some pastors provide a kind objectivity that helps people separate reasoned arguments from prejudice, so that decisions may be reached rationally. Others have tried to sort out the causes of conflicts, which may reach back some years into the history of the relationships among the participants. They have tried to unravel the causes of conflict, much as a psychoanalyst seeks to sort out the causes of a personal character disorder. Other pastors have seen the goal-setting process fall victim to sharp differences in a congregation that long preceded the advent of any particular program—if one family was favorable, another family was already opposed! Some pastors have outlived the combatants. Others have simply withdrawn and looked for a call to another congregation.

Some small congregations have been helpful in humanizing young pastors beyond any education our seminaries can offer.

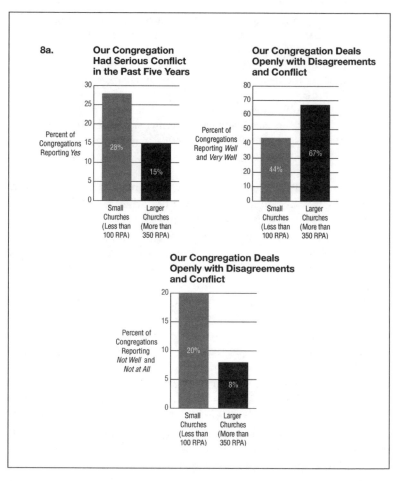

8a.

Our Congregation Had Serious Conflict in the Past Five Years

Percent of Congregations Reporting *Yes*

- Small Churches (Less than 100 RPA): 28%
- Larger Churches (More than 350 RPA): 15%

Our Congregation Deals Openly with Disagreements and Conflict

Percent of Congregations Reporting *Well* and *Very Well*

- Small Churches (Less than 100 RPA): 44%
- Larger Churches (More than 350 RPA): 67%

Our Congregation Deals Openly with Disagreements and Conflict

Percent of Congregations Reporting *Not Well* and *Not at All*

- Small Churches (Less than 100 RPA): 20%
- Larger Churches (More than 350 RPA): 8%

However, a few congregations have a record of doing the opposite. They seem to chew up pastors, the old and the young alike. This second kind of congregation seems to be composed of families who have agreed to disagree vehemently but passively. Among themselves, they have developed a social sickness we might call "symbiotic animosity": they have learned to enjoy mutual enmity. In Coser's words, they need "hate objects," but not victory.[7] Among themselves, they have evolved a relationship of cool cordiality that masks their hostility. But woe to the program that gets tossed up between these families: they will destroy it. Woe to the unsuspecting pastor who tries to sort it out rationally. In Coser's terms, some families seem to "enjoy hating" each other, and the new pastor is grist for the mill. He or she should not assume the burden of "failure" if the cause of the conflict long preceded the pastor's arrival.

Coser's insights should not be lost: stable small churches are free to fight. For the most part, the pastor does not cause the conflict. The new pastor is simply not that important, at least in the first few years. The conflict "teams" were usually aligned long before the pastor arrived (although there are always exceptional pastors who do precipitate fights—sometimes wherever they go). The pastor must be in touch with his or her personal feelings and be professionally prepared to seek a more durable settlement.

Pastor as Sportscaster

Pastors should do more than tolerate conflict and survive. They should find constructive ways to use it to help congregations see themselves more clearly, and move on with their ministries. Recent leadership analysts have been especially helpful in providing guidelines to help congregations learn from their experiences.[8] Ronald Heifetz has identified strategies that are particularly useful for pastors in small churches who want to make constructive use of their natural conflicts. Rather than repress or deny the conflict, Heifetz helps adaptive leaders create a safe place for exploring tensions and differences, what he calls a "scaffolding for creativity."[9] In a similar approach from case studies in ministry, Jackson W. Carroll offers religious leaders a contemporary and constructive design for leadership in what he calls a "post traditional world." [10] While affirming that the office of clergy has declined in social status, Carroll describes the new authority some clergy have achieved as "reflective practitioners" who help the congregation to see themselves more clearly as carriers of the sacred in a secular world.

Popular clergy images have struggled to capture this leadership style by borrowing from the sports arena, suggesting that the clergy should think of themselves as referees who enforce the rules, or as coaches who nurture players and direct the game. In the same vein, one significant role model for pastors—especially in the natural conflicts of small churches—is the "sportscaster." When I approached some small church pastors about this image for their work, one pastor protested that he wanted to become "not just the play-by-play announcer, but the color commentator who explains the background and finer points of the game, and observes how well the team is doing." In the process, the sportscaster does not aspire to be either owner or manager, but uses the clergy office to raise congregational sensitivity about their behavior and its implications. Conflicts are often so "scripted" that, in setting their goals, the leaders are already aware of their teams, for example, if the A Team is in favor of the proposal, the B Team will oppose it, and the C Team will not play. Pastors have agreed that "sportscasters are much needed, to reflect back to our congregations the games that they are playing—and ask them if that's what the Lord wants here and now."

Sportscaster is a strong role for clergy who are willing to deal with small-church conflict. It takes disciplines of observation, timing, and courage to become a first-rate sportscaster who explains to the congregation the games they are playing among themselves, and with the larger world. When sportscaster is combined with pastor as lover (as suggested in chapter 4), it provides the combination of objectivity and intimacy necessary for leadership—neither self-image alone is sufficient for the task. With data from FACT congregations, we see that congregations reporting serious conflicts are far less likely to report that they are "spiritually vital and alive." At the same time, this negative condition is reversed if congregations can "deal with conflict openly." (Fig. 8b) The task of the sportscaster-lover is not to manage or repress "natural conflicts" of small churches, but to transform them into constructive events.

Goals and Purposes

Despite these liabilities and land mines, clarifying goals is one effective means to help a small congregation to mobilize its positive strength. As one pastor said in review of a year's work in order to sharpen the goals of the church: "For years, the church had existed with each member assuming that he knew what the others felt. Now, they had the opportunity to express themselves.

They experienced a oneness in the Lord. Spiritually, it was a healthy experience."

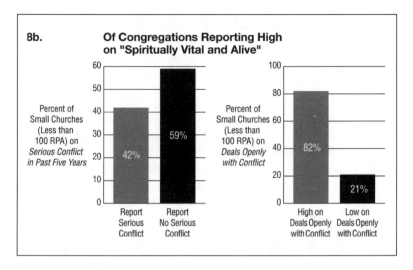

Goal setting works when the small church feels the time is right. Clarity of goals cannot be the agenda of the pastor only, it must also belong to the people. Goal setting can be helpful when:

- Not everyone is expected to participate in the same way.
- Identity from the past is foundational, not forgotten.
- The present situation is seen as an opportunity, not a threat.
- Decisions are made more by consensus than by vote.
- Program responsibilities are not always processed through organizational assignment.

The relational style of many small congregations finds expression in governing by "adhocracy": "He who will, let him respond."

In a small church, these values are likely to be expressed differently in several significant ways. First, the small church tends to be more conserving. As Alice Mann makes clear in her eminently useful guide,[11] members of small churches want to see the relationship between church purposes and organizational goals. The more they treasure their experience in the past, the more they will want to see the connection between the proposed church goals and the proud history of the church. Goal setting is not just an organizational program; it must be a spiritual experience. The effects are noticeable first in the enthusiasm of congregational worship, and therefore prayer and reflection should provide the spiritual context for developing common goals.

Second, older members in the congregation will play an affirming and surprising role. Unlike the age distribution in many larger congregations, in small churches the elderly are usually present and vocal. Often they have lived through several cycles of church membership, and they know the crosses that members still carry. They have seen pastors come and go, and remember "how we got to where we are." Older members offer two kinds of contributions to the process of congregational renewal. On the one hand, they honor the traditions but do not cling too closely to them. Younger church officers often want to "do things right." Often the elderly, given the opportunity to reflect, can have a wider perspective. They know that we did not always do it this way. Further, in personal terms, the matriarchs and patriarchs can manage the first sergeants, when necessary. On the other hand, the elderly can provide a substitute source for the new ideas that other congregations may receive from a flow of new members. The elderly have imagination. They remember the images and models of the past when "we did it differently in Reverend Jones's time." In many small congregations, the elderly offer the most liberated source for innovative alternatives to current programs. What's more, when the old-timers are deeply committed to the new in the name of the old, who is going to argue with their memories?

Third, the number of goals chosen in a small church is different, for goals serve opposite functions in large and small churches. The large church will typically choose many major goals, smaller goals, objectives, and tasks. For the larger congregation, multiple goals provide the banners around which to rally the support of each of many different church groups. Multiple goals provide an appropriate basis for the several interest groups and tasks groups that make a larger church effective. Through many groups, it can absorb more people. The small church typically chooses fewer and different goals, for the opposite reason. In the small church, the goals must serve to unify the congregation, not divide it. In other words, in the large church the whole congregation accepts the process and tolerates a diversity of goals. In a small congregation, the church accepts all of the goals, but only tolerates the process. What appears to be the same procedure serves opposite functions in larger and smaller congregations.

Fourth, small churches find more of their goals in what they are already doing. In large congregations, goal setting often produces a whole harvest of new ideas. In the small church, the process often allows the congregation to hear themselves say what is important, so that they can concentrate their resources to do it better. The large congregation needs quantity to keep going. The small church provides a different quality of care. Thus, the exercise at the beginning of this chapter often provides a flow of ideas: what is our purpose, formal and informal? What are we doing well, and what could we be doing better? In the panorama of our possibilities, where is there a place for innovation? When is it time to let something go? Church goals and purposes should judge the quality of church groups, and the real life of the groups should refine the accuracy of church goals. Matching should provide a simple way to view the strength of church life in an effective small church—in quality, not quantity.

"Do half as much, twice as well," was the mantra of one young pastor, and in the process she was able to attract her generational peers of boomers and Xers. Out of her own experience in trying to balance being pastor and mother, she recognized the hunger for Sabbath, a spiritual quest unsatisfied by ever more activity.[12] Hers is a congregation with unusual emphasis on "open spaces of time" not only in worship, but in their programs, and in the way they decide what programs to organize.

Throughout the formal process, in the small church there is a much shorter loop between the perception of need and the capacity to respond. One pastor voices the experience of many: "When people see the human need, they have fantastic resources." Unfortunately, the inverse is also true: when people get discouraged, they become legalistic, demanding, and negative. Discouragement leads to despondency. The effective small church has found a way to use the short feedback loop to its advantage. They celebrate their victories. They feel a need, fill it, and then they celebrate. They celebrate because it feels good to be helpful. They come to think of themselves as helpful, sensitive to needs that can be filled. A wedding anniversary can be a cause for celebration, or a church dinner, the birth of a child, the end of school (or the return to school), the return of someone from sickness, a letter from a friend, or even the death of a life well lived.[13] In the small church, "if one member suffers, all suffer together with it; if one member is honored, all rejoice together with it" (1 Cor. 12:26).

The appropriate affirmation of purpose and clarity of goals should be an aid to the leadership of small congregations. It should support, but never inhibit, the spontaneous sharing of mundane victories and the quality of caring for people and parish, through which God liberates people from a sense of anonymous helplessness in the blur of the mass society.

Suggestions for Further Reading

Carroll, Jackson W. *As One with Authority: Reflective Leadership in Ministry.* Louisville, Ky.: Westminster/John Knox Press, 1991.
  Authenticity for clergy in the twenty-first century.

Crandall, Ron. *Turnaround Strategies for the Small Church.* Nashville: Abingdon Press, 1995.
  Biblical and challenging strategy for revitalizing congregations.

Heifetz, Ronald A. *Leadership without Easy Answers.* Cambridge, Mass.: Harvard University Press, 1994.
  A foundational leadership strategy that fits small churches.

Mann, Alice. *Can Our Church Live?: Redeveloping Congregations in Decline.* Bethesda, Md.: Alban Institute, 1999.
  Renewal at a pace that every church can do it.

CHAPTER NINE EXERCISE
Ministry Map

In this exercise, lay and clergy (if available) work together to draw a rough area map of your primary ministry that locates your members and identifies other major populations that share your space.[1] Begin with a blank sheet of newsprint fixed on the wall that is sufficiently large to be seen from a distance (maybe 36 inches square, or larger). Locate the church building somewhere near the center, and enter the major streets and arterial highways that define your space. Add the natural boundaries and barriers, such as rivers and railways, hills and valleys, that clearly locate your church and its community. For some city areas, the map may be only a few blocks, for suburban or rural congregations it may include a much larger area. Members of your congregation should immediately recognize the primary features without adding every detail of neighboring streets and familiar landmarks.

Now enter information about the people who live there. Begin by locating your own members on the map, at least the most active families. You can add interest by using different color dots for families who have joined in different decades. The color pattern will immediately indicate where the older members live, and areas from which newer members are coming.

When the members have been located, identify on your map the various neighborhoods that are included in your ministry area. Are some areas more likely to have apartments and others single family homes? You might want to locate the commercial and industrial space, but think primarily about the population groups. Designate neighborhoods that are dominated by an eth-

153

nic, religious, or other group, such as Korean, Catholic, or gay. Are there particular areas of housing for people with low incomes, while other sections attract high-income households? Where do the older citizens live, and where are the young families? Do neighborhoods have nicknames, and are those designations still accurate? You should check the accuracy of your memories, and then enter the appropriate designations on your map.

To sensitize your members to community social issues, designate who you think might be "invisible people," that is, population groups who have been overlooked, neglected, and marginalized in your community, such as the elderly or young single people. As you enter the names of groups in various areas, mark the "invisible people" in red, and include them in your prayer concerns.

To enliven your map, add personal or newspaper pictures of members, places, or events in various parts of the community.

Energizing from Within

Church size, even in small churches, is not the *only* factor that shapes how congregations will behave. Smaller congregations generally share the values of personal satisfactions among members and focus on congregational activity. In the member satisfactions, small congregations typically have much more in common with small congregations of other denominations than they have with larger churches in their community or in their denomination. But size is not the only, or always the most important, factor that shapes the character of a particular congregation.

To find out what defined a church, we asked the members. Most people, if they gave any response at all, pointed to the objective facts of their history and their location, saying "We're the Methodist Church at this end of town." When asked why they attend, most people respond with a subjective judgment of personal satisfaction or faith conviction, "I like the worship and the people here." When asked why they chose a particular congregation, most people remember the invitation of a relative or friend, "Suzanne brought me here in the fall, about five years ago." These elements of objective data, personal judgment, and social relationships become mixed to determine the lifestyle of a particular congregation. Like individual people, the congregation has a character composed of its past experiences and personal expectations. With such a mixture, we know that no two churches are alike, and any particular congregation will never exactly fit the categories that we offer to understand and energize church behavior.

Church size is most helpful when it is seen as one dimension among other forces that shape the church and affect its character. Size has about the same influence on the character of a church that it has on the self-image of a person—it is more important for some people than for others, and important some times and not others. We will consider three other formative influences: congregational heritage, life cycle, and social location. Together they suggest a rough typology that helps us see significant differences among small churches. Such a sorting out of characteristics should help small congregations discover Kindred Spirits, learn from those who are different, and raise their own commitments toward a higher quality of Christian caring in their own way.

Congregational Heritage

Each small church inherits self-images and expectations that directly effect the lifestyle of the congregation. In a broad sense, denominational labels have historical (even biological) connections that carry cultural-theological implications. Many denominations have roots in particular national immigrant groups—Scandinavians were Lutheran; Irish, Catholics; Scottish, Presbyterians; and so on. These historic ties are cultural as well as theological, that is, their faith has been carried by their culture. In addition, these denominational ties provided church organization and polity, liturgy and educational literature, trained clergy and membership expectations, and a long history of interrelationships between each of these traditions and the culture where it was located.

Even if this inheritance is rejected or denied, these historical roots are deeply embedded and usually provide the framework for whatever actions the local church may take. H. Richard Niebuhr has contributed two classic studies that interpret this inheritance: in *Social Sources of Denominationalism* he outlines (and partially laments) our denominational differences. In *Christ and Culture,* he suggests a scheme to appreciate and integrate five distinct streams of denominational tradition in the early twentieth century.[2]

Different streams of tradition can be carried not only between churches, but also within a single denomination. Avery Dulles,

S. J., has shown the existence of multiple "models" (understand-ings) of the church within the Catholic tradition,[3] each with the deep commitment of its supporters. Although more than half of the small churches are fiercely "independent" of any denomina-tional tradition, their independence becomes itself a tradition.[4] No congregation invents its faith *de novo*, but each must find new ways to translate that inheritance into forms that seem appropri-ate for its particular setting.

Life Cycle

Congregations also have an organizational history that follows what some have called a "life cycle." In an effort to help congre-gations reignite the passion of their early years, to "dream again," Robert Dale defined the life experiences of a congregation in five stages: birth, growth, maturity, decline, and death.[5] Dale used a bell curve to describe the increasing energy that can be experi-enced as the congregation moves from dream to belief to goals to structure into ministry. He then described the decline as nostalgia to questioning to polarization to drop out and organizational death. To counter this "natural curve," Dale proposes a new plan-ning "cycle" that must recur and reenergize the church much like the season of the year.

Others have created their own variations and strategies for dealing with the sequence of birth and formation, stability and redefinition, decline and redevelopment.[6] Clearly, many small congregations have survived the transition of several generations, and they can look back to former leaders who found ways "to dream again." At the same time, the challenge is con-stantly renewed. As one old veteran told me, "We are always only a generation from disappearing, but somehow we survive . . . so far." FACT data confirm the struggle to maintain a focus against the accumulation of the years, plus the additional challenge that a clear vision is about equally difficult in various social locations.

Social Location

Most church leaders, consultants, and authors rely on social location to explain the behavior of particular congregations.[7] This

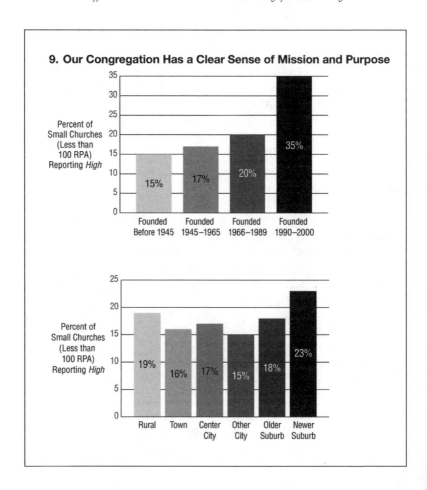

9. Our Congregation Has a Clear Sense of Mission and Purpose

Percent of Small Churches (Less than 100 RPA) Reporting *High*

- Founded Before 1945: 15%
- Founded 1945–1965: 17%
- Founded 1966–1989: 20%
- Founded 1990–2000: 35%

Percent of Small Churches (Less than 100 RPA) Reporting *High*

- Rural: 19%
- Town: 16%
- Center City: 17%
- Other City: 15%
- Older Suburb: 18%
- Newer Suburb: 23%

literature assumes that the social location of the congregation shapes the type of Christian witness that will be effective. Douglas Walrath in his often-quoted essay, "Types of Small Congregations and Their Implications for Planning,"[8] describes twelve types of social context, each with demographic characteristics, patterns of population change, and typical church profiles. The twelve locales are designated: mid-town, inner city, inner-urban neighborhood, outer-urban neighborhood, city suburb, metropolitan suburb, fringe suburb, fringe village, fringe settlement, independent city, rural village, and rural settlement. The logical progression and supporting data provide an orderly framework for considering the importance of each environment on the nature of particular churches.

But in the dynamics of American demography, populations often change—cities spawn new suburbs, rural areas may decline in numbers (and increase in wealth), highways make some towns obsolete and create new centers. Within these dynamics, characteristics of populations may change with immigrant groups, internal migration, shift stylishness of particular neighborhoods, and the universal process of family life cycles, even when the individuals stay put. As our communities are constantly changing, churches have difficulty in continuing to reach the new population with an appealing message. Other studies have responded to the problems facing congregations caught in communities in transition.[9] But in the lives of congregations, these elements of congregational heritage, life cycle and social location are woven together. In *Parish Planning*, Lyle Schaller offers such a tapestry:

> Today, even an elementary listing of the categories of church types would include the metropolitan church . . . , the downtown "First Church". . . , the neighborhood church in the central city or older suburb . . . , the nationality or language congregation, the black church . . . , the "gathered congregation" that is trying to perpetuate yesterday, the specialized urban congregation, such as the university church, the intentional nongeographical urban parish, the "Memorial" church dominated for decades by one person or one family, the new suburban mission, the church in a racially changing community, the long-established congregation on the rural-urban fringe, the fifteen- or twenty-year-old suburban congregation, the "First Church" in the county seat town, the small, open-country congregation, the church in the small trading center, and the church in the dying crossroads village.[10]

Schaller further suggests, "It is also possible to cut the cake in another direction and to define such categories as the growing congregation, the family church, the dying church, the subsidized church, the church in mission, and the churches which . . . minister to certain distinctive life styles in society."

I believe that the most helpful way to appreciate the congregational commitments lies in the comparison among congregations based on the attitude of the members toward the place where the church is located. The combination of faith and place, yet sensitive to life cycle, produces "turf types" of congregations. Without violating the most fundamental uniqueness that is the character of each congregation, church types based on turf commitments may provide a basis for small churches to see themselves more clearly and claim their ministries more fully.

Turf Types: Regional and Local

A council member of a large parish once described turf types of churches that participated in the council. He said: "We all gather in our churches, but we gather differently. One church is a gathering *in* the community, and another is the gathering *of* the whole community. One of the churches gathers *from* the community, and others gather *from several* communities. The last church is a gathering of an *ethnic 'clan'* who live throughout the whole area. They meet in an open country church, and everyone is welcome who can find it, and speaks 'Dutch' [Deutsch]."

These different ways that churches gather provide the basis for a typology of small congregations. For our purpose, the attitudes of people toward the turf of the church can be separated into two broad categories. Some people attend a church that draws its membership from throughout the region. They share a faith based on their common cultural heritage, their denominational commitments, or their personal Christian experience. They are not confined to a specific geography or "parish boundaries," but have a concern to attract like-minded people from throughout the area. They are *regional churches.*

Other people choose a church that has a more specific and identifiable geographic base. They gather in a church that is "of" the community, or at least it is "in" the community. Cultural and denominational interests are secondary to sharing the faith with people with whom they share the community. Their sense of church turf is local and defined by specific boundaries. They may not be able to share their particular faith with everyone in that turf, but they share with them a concern for everything that happens in that space. It is their common parish.

Regional churches and parish churches reflect a basic difference in the way people gather into congregations. But within each of these two broad categories, several distinctions must be made. We shall discuss three kinds of regional appeals. One is the *Old First Church* of the denomination, the first, clearest, and most proper expression of that faith group in the area. A second regional church is represented in the *ethnic congregation,* which is open to anyone who can find it and speaks its language. The third regional appeal is found in the *high-commitment congregations* who base their faith primarily on personal conviction and private experience. These three kinds of congregations all draw members from regional areas. All three may show the same total membership, but they have vastly different styles of Christian life and witness. They may be of the same denomination and/or from the same social location, but they simply "gather differently."

By comparison, we will consider three attitudes toward the turf that may be found in local parish churches. The basic attitude is that they belong to the land, and the land belongs to them. The first type of parish is *stable.* Unfortunately, there are not many stable communities. The neighborhood church is affected by two additional attitudes toward their parish turf. One is positive, which anticipates *growth* in the population of "our sort of people." The Protestant church has demonstrated a remarkable aptitude for helping our new families in growing communities assimilate into the fabric of the neighborhood. We have recorded this as church growth. The other attitude toward change in the church turf is negative. It anticipates a *decline* in the population of our people, hence a decrease in the number of prospective members of the congregation. Thus, neighborhood churches view their parish as stable, growing, or declining. The way they perceive their relationship to the land will shape the self-image and program options for the congregation. To broaden the base of understanding, we will include parallel self-images of congregations from a more recent study that examined church participation in community outreach ministries. Although generated from the stories that churches told about themselves, these images are remarkably similar to the turf types we propose.[11]

Regional: Holy Trinity or Old First: The Pillar Church

Old First Church does things properly, with style. It may have a tall steeple, a high pulpit, a pipe organ, a robed choir, and invitations to the Internet—even if only twenty-five people attend. Old First is the voice and witness of the denomination. The congregation can appeal to people from throughout the region, regardless of their ethnic, racial, or economic background. Members tend toward educational similarities and often have old family ties. These churches are the denominational cathedrals that gather those who appreciate "the best."

Old First does not solicit for members, but absorbs new people through a process of adoption. Prospective members are often attracted by the quality of special programs that Old First provides. Budget in Old First often comes from endowment. Yet membership will contribute to maintain a proud ministry when asked at a congregational community dinner or through mail solicitation. The fine line between church concerns and community concerns is never precise, and community groups often meet in the church buildings. Although it is clear that many of the community leaders belong to Old First, it is not always clear who does not belong. One pastor of Old First noted that the "work of the church is easily shared with many people who are not officially members, but they care." He noted that community people have often been the "backbone of our church-sponsored community ministry." In another study, we called these congregations "pillar churches."

*The **pillar church** is anchored in its community, a place for which it feels a distinct responsibility. The architecture often reflects this self-image—strong pillars that lift the roof physically and the community spiritually. The building may be modest in a small town or imposing in a neighborhood that expects a prominent architectural posture. Like the building, the members are pillars of the community, good citizens individually and corporately. More than the building, they share a Pillar mindset. Resources of heritage, leadership, facilities, and finances are used to strengthen the whole community (1 Peter 2:4-10).*[12]

Regional: Ethnic Family: The Pilgrim Church

The ethnic church is a cultural family at prayer. When they gather, time stands still. They have a wide building, a variety of musical instruments, several strong singers (or several choirs), a charismatic leader, and no printed program at all. The choreography and momentum of their worship is every bit as old and fixed as the worship in Old First Church, but very different. They may have a turf association with a particular building where they worship. Or they may share a memory of a place that was long ago in their lives—a town in the south, a valley in Puerto Rico, a village in the old country. The roots to their culture are often stronger than denominational connections. One pastor wonders, "Since the church has moved so often, I fear that our people are more loyal to culture or rather to an ethnic God, one that is present only in their particular language and their form of worship."

Ethnic churches receive new members by adoption into the larger family. The same pastor envied the importance of the church in the lives of the members, old and new: "They belong to the church and become part of its life, and it becomes a part of them." New members often discover the church through annual events and family crises. In ethnic churches, there are many "annual members" and no sustained effort to distinguish between church membership and family caring. One pastor of a historic black church reported that his church achieved positive results when he began to pastor without a membership roll. "Evangelism," he said, "begins with pastoral care. We came alive when we made unofficial members of everyone who shared in the ministry of the church. Our caring was done mostly through church families anyway."

The absence of clear membership lists makes pledging difficult, but it extends the family to include a much larger constituency. In addition, about 25 percent of the income for this congregation was raised in popular annual events, which also attracted a much larger constituency. Ethnic congregations can perceive themselves as oppressed minorities, sometimes accurately, but other times this attitude appears to be a residual from early periods of struggle and deprivation. They have a well-earned reputation for survival in the midst of adversity. Since they are on a pilgrimage journey with their members, we called them *pilgrim churches*.

*The **pilgrim church** takes care of its own people wherever they are, as distinguished from the pillar church's sense of being rooted in place. Some pilgrim congregations have moved with their people, from one dwelling place to another. Their culture and their Christian faith are woven in a single fabric of their lives. They may not have a strong sense of universal justice, but they react with high commitment when they perceive injustice or deprivation among one of their own. Some older pilgrim congregations have seen waves of immigrant or racial change, and old and new ethnics, and they use their sense of Christian pilgrimage to reach out to include the most recent "stranger" in their midst (Hebrews 11:13, 1 Peter 2:9).*

Regional: High-commitment: The Prophetic Church

High-commitment congregations are a mountain of energy determined to move the world by faith. They often articulate clearly the meaning of membership and the mission of the church. Members make substantial commitments of time and resources to witness their faith and achieve their stated goals. The intensity of their commitment provides a sharp contrast and a viable alternative to more traditional churches. They are gathered from the world and for the world.

Membership in a high-commitment congregation is a personal decision involving self-denial and discipline. Prospective members learn about the work of the church through reputation. High-commitment congregations place a premium on the articulation of their faith. They often publish their own materials or purchase them from independent sources. Old First Church seeks a kind of denominational purity, the ethnic congregation expresses a cultural purity, and the high-commitment church expects a personal religious purity. Because of the clarity of their faith and the energy of their activities, high-commitment churches often attract disproportionate attention from the media, casting a negative shadow on other kinds of small churches.

In fund raising, they are clearly unique: only tithes, gifts, and offerings—no bazaars or cookie sales. They often focus their attention on particular spiritual and social problems in the community, for which they organize a program that they staff by their own volunteer members. High-commitment congregations often locate in communities where their help is needed, but they deny that the place of worship has any significance for them. The funds of these congregations, which are not sustained by either turf or tradition, last as long as the commitments of the members. Because their call is to renew the covenant, we have also called these "prophetic churches."[13]

*The **prophetic church** understands its calling to challenge the world, which may focus on many expressions of evil from individuals to corporations, from communities to nations. Independent, often entrepreneurial in style, these crusaders are supported by people who share their commitments. Both prophetic churches and survivor churches (see below) carry a sense of crisis and expect a high-energy response, but the prophetic are pro-active while the survivors are reactive. These high-profile congregations, whether large or small, often have an unusual impact and set the standards for other congregations (Great commandment and commission, Micah 6:8).*

Local: Stable Conditions: The Servant Church

The stable parish provides the model of turf identification: the church is a gathering in the community and of the community. The church and community share a concern for the families and individuals who live there, and for the resources that make a community viable. The stable community church reflects the interdependence of families and the soil, which have cared for each other for several generations. For better or for worse, few such idyllic communities exist in the economy of our land.

We are a mobile nation, and no community is exempt from change. Family farms and decentralized industry have allowed some rural families to stay on their land and to support the neighboring economy. Some metropolitan communities have remained relatively stable if anchored in common ethnic ties and parochial, middle-class institutions. There appears to be relatively little mobility at the extreme ends of the economy: the landed gentry and the persistently poor. The appearance of stability in other communities often masks the quiet, short hops that families make up the rungs of their dream of economic success. Statistically, the populations appear the same. Only the people have moved; about half of them move every five years.

Typically, the church in the stable community has a widely scattered and aging membership. The church must work hard to keep up with the changes, stay even in membership, and reach the people who might respond to their invitation. The church community is not easily defined. It is a geographic area, but not everyone in that area will respond. It is a community of faith, but never limited to those who have made a confession. In rural areas, the parish may pulsate with the influx of seasonal residents. In urban areas, the weekday contacts among members may become less frequent and more difficult. The church community is increasingly difficult to define and to reach with the gospel.

Effective churches in relatively stable communities usually become identified with the community groups that use their buildings. One urban pastor describes a strategy of using neighborhood buildings for church projects and encouraging the neighborhood groups to use the church building. He called it "getting the church into the community, and the community into the church." Even the church in the stable community cannot simply wait to be found by the community. Based on histories of caring congregations embedded in their communities, we have called these *servant churches*.

The **servant church** *goes about the work of helping people in need with quiet faithfulness. These churches are neither threatened nor assertive. Where pillar churches feel responsible for the whole community and pilgrim churches respond to particular groups of people, servants see individuals in need and reach out to help them in supportive and pastoral ways. Servant churches are sustained by servant people— those who visit the sick, take meals to the bereaved, and send cards to shut-ins. From there, it is a natural extension to provide food, clothing, and other basic needs to their neighbors. Their faith is lived out in service (Mark 9:35, Acts 2:45).*

Local: Growing Context: The Intentional Church

When the community is expanding, or when the population is turning over rapidly, the *intentional church* provides services that newcomers need and appreciate. On the one hand, they assimilate families rapidly into the friendship fabric of the community. On the other hand, they provide the necessary connections with family doctors, automobile repair shops, hardware stores for hard-to-find items, and dentists for the inevitable check-up. The church can help the transplanted family take root in the community. With minimum effort and organization, churches in growing communities have thrived.

In many ways, they resemble the high-commitment congregation. They are intentional about their activities and concentrate on specific community concerns, such as day care facilities, youth programs, and mental health. Funds are pledged annually, often by telephone canvass of the congregation. They have a clear sense of their mission.

As one pastor says, "We need a mission to stay alive." He goes on: "We know that we are not the most important group in the community, but we are important to each other. If we stopped serving others, we would smother to death." Not mission, but financial commitments usually precipitate a felt need for more members. But some have resisted the natural inclination to add members, and chose to intensify their commitments. We call them "intentional (small) churches."[14]

*The **intentional church** chooses not to increase beyond a fixed membership of about one hundred or perhaps one hundred fifty people. They reflect many of the positive community values of trained leadership, efficient planning, easily digested materials, measurable results, and continual evaluation. But they have made a conscious decision not to grow beyond the number of people who can keep in touch with one another, who can know one another personally. They replace members who move away, but they have not grown beyond the single caring cell (Mark 8:31-9:1).*

Local: Declining Area: The Survivor Church

"Why can't they be like us?"[15] is the challenging title of Andrew Greeley's hard-hitting study of white ethnic consciousness in mobile America. The recognition that "they" and "us" are different creates the most perplexing problem that confronts the witness of small churches. Communities are often increasing in total population; but when the newcomers are not responsive to "our" sorts of churches, the neighborhood is seen to be "declining" by the members of the church. Because of cultural differences in religious expression, the church is caught in an apparently impossible choice: It will not succeed in attracting people simply by trying a little harder. It might reach new people if it changed its program and approach, but the changes might alienate the members who remain. To keep their scattered members, they need excellent transportation and an unusually appealing program. To survive the cultural transition, they need a substantial investment of human energy and financial resources. Even then, a happy ending is not assured.

Churches in "declining" neighborhoods feel that their turf has been invaded or drained. Too often they have been driven indoors, with an edifice complex about their building and a series of storm appeals for money. Further, the congregation often carries grief for lost members whom the most recent pastor does not know and has never met. Even if they are successful in reaching a few of the new population who have moved into the community, they often discover that the people who have responded to them are the most dissimilar to the other recent arrivals. The first of the newcomers to join are often the least able to reach the others, and the least interested in trying.

Churches that perceive their communities as declining are typically located in older residential areas of the city or on the rural-metropolitan fringe. Both see themselves as islands of faithful witness in a sea of human need and religious indifference. Although the populations may be growing, both congregations perceive their communities as declining because "our sort of people" are not moving in. Churches on the rural-metropolitan fringe have discovered great differences in program and pace between families who have lived in a community all their lives, and those who are relatively recent arrivals. To reach the new residents, fringe churches must accelerate the pace of the program.

Small churches in the city are often faced with the opposite situation. Both church and community have usually aged together, offering opportunities for service primarily among an elderly, more casual population. To provide needed care, many urban congregations have slowed down their pace and expanded their hours. One city pastor described the turning point: "We concentrated on the elderly, widows, and widowers. We started where we hurt the worst, and these 'people issues' touched other people. Since they got turned on, the response has been overwhelming." Churches in changing communities can be amazingly effective when they hunker down and turn their crisis into a virtue. We called these *survivor churches.*

The **survivor church** *tells of the storms it has weathered. Often the congregation attracts and sustains people who take pride in their survival, like the endurance on the cross. Survivor churches live on the edge, always on the verge of being overwhelmed by emergencies. They do not expect to conquer their problems, but they will not give in. They are determined rather than relentless or aggressive. They hang on because "we've made it through worse than this before." Although outsiders may see these churches as "weak," they can be resilient, productive, and loving when leaders learn to make positive use of their orientation to crises (Matthew 7:24-7, 1 Corinthians 4:12).*

Small churches share common commitment to caring for one another, but they go about it very differently.

Reflecting Your Church's Image

Your map should now serve as a mirror to see more clearly the way (or perhaps the combination of ways) that your congregation relates to its turf. Simply the size of the area that you chose to include in the map will suggest if you should consider yourself a regional church. How much territory do you consider your area of ministry? Regional churches will embrace a larger space; local churches will concentrate their attention (although some faithful souls will drive amazing distances "religiously" every week, or more often, to be with a neighborhood church they dearly love).

Then look for clues in your building, your physical church. First Churches are marked not only by the pillars that sustain the porch, but also by the pristine manner in which the property is maintained. In most First Church buildings, you see the symbols and often the design of their denominational heritage, right down to the color scheme that is consistent with their cultural and religious heritage. By contrast, for example, the prophetic church tends toward symbols of the high priority that they place on mission, and as a result they will permit (or even encourage) the building to appear "a bit run-down" to confirm their alternate values. The location of the building will also suggest the congregation's self image—regional churches will need to have access to arterial highways, while neighborhood churches are more comfortable being tucked away on side streets.

Your map will tell you even more when posted side-by-side with your earlier exercises of a congregational time line, the stories associated with "silent history," and your calendar of annual church events.[16] In the stories you have elicited while building these materials, you should have seen your self-image more clearly reflected. Pilgrim (ethnic) churches, for example, take special interest in blood and family ties, pausing in a story to explain the specific links by which the characters are related; "You know, he's old John's eldest brother." Survivor churches, on the other hand, keep reminding the listeners that this story is as terribly important as their most recent crisis, and your help is needed to meet the new (and continuing) emergency.

Together, the exercises at the beginning of this chapter should suggest some of the bridges that connect you to your community, and some of the barriers that inhibit your neighbors from attending. By "bridges" we mean the celebrations and struggles that the church has shared with the community over the years. By "barriers" we mean the disconnections between the internal life of the congregation and the faith journeys of your neighbors and colleagues in your space.

Your map will also suggest "bridge people" who may be able to use their current and past connections to renew relationships with your community. An amazing array of people will respond when church members go visiting with neighbors in their communities—shopkeepers and educators, police officers and hairstylists, caregivers and reporters, old friends and acquaintances. Listen with them as your share your stories, for the way you tell your story permits the bridges to be rebuilt in worship, in small groups, and in your annual events.[17]

Mobilizing Image Energy

Comparisons between these turf types of churches should help congregations mobilize energy from knowing who they are, and not trying to act from an image that does not suit them. In small-church workshops, pastors say their congregations show different levels of activity that reflect their own self-image.[18] When asked about specific attendance at various functions, pastors and church leaders reported the following as percent of members attending:

	Average Worship Attendance	Fellowship Groups Participation	Annual/Special Events
Old First Church - *Pillar*	30% of members	50% of members	80% members + guests
Ethnic church - *Pilgrim*	50%	30%	120% +friends
High-commitment church *Prophetic*	70%	80%	90%
Stable parish church *Servant*	35%	50%	60% + guests
Growing-community church - *Intentional*	40% + visitors	60% + visitors	80% + visitors
Declining-community church - *Survivor*	25%	30%	40%

Particular turf types can be compared in the many different ways that they witness to their distinctive interpretation of the Christian faith. With pastors we noted a few similarities and differences concerning fund-raising, membership recruitment and participation, and community service. These congregations can also be compared in worship and liturgy; in leadership styles and recruitment; in their annual and special events; and in their sense of place, pace, history, and architecture.[19] The comparisons are endless, instructive, and fun.

Laity, I find, can compare these types with greater clarity than can the ordained clergy. Perhaps the clergy have been called to serve a generic definition of "the church universal," while laity have chosen freely the particular church that best expresses who they are.

Church types are important because they help identify appropriate programs and relieve the anxiety created by inappropriate expectations. Knowing the character of our church allows us to have confidence in our decisions and to articulate our identity with such clarity that outsiders can be clear about the church they are joining. But even more, the recognition of our own identity helps us discover how much we need one another. No one type, no one theology, and no one denomination can do it alone. In confessing our uniqueness, we discover how much we need others to find the fullness of the Body of Christ.

Suggestions for Further Reading

Dudley, Carl S. and Sally A. Johnson. *Energizing the Congregation: Images that Shape Your Church's Ministry.* Louisville: Westminster/ John Knox, 1993.
    Self-images from congregational stories.

Pelton, Robert S., ed. *Small Christian Communities: Imagining Future Church.* Notre Dame, Ind.: University of Notre Dame Press, 1997.
    Insights from intentionally small churches.

Wilkes, Paul. *Excellent Protestant Congregations: The Guide to Best Places and Practices.* Louisville: Westminster/John Knox, 2001.
    Overview of 300 congregations with case studies and best practices.

Wimberly, Edward P. *Recalling Our Own Stories: Spiritual Renewal for Religious Caregivers.* San Francisco: Jossey-Bass, 1997.
    Making clear and useful what we used to do naturally.

Church in Community Map

This exercise is similar to the previous one in that you begin by preparing a rough map of the area of your primary ministry.[1] You can begin with another blank sheet of newsprint fixed on the wall (maybe 36 inches square, or larger) to create a second map similar to the first, or you can add this information directly on your first map if it is not already too cluttered. In either case, your church building should appear somewhere near the center, and be surrounded by easily identifiable major streets, highways, and natural boundaries that identify your area. When seen by members of your congregation, they should immediately recognize the primary features.

The Church in Community Map will move the focus from the people of your community to the institutions, agencies, and associations that make things happen—and all your potential allies and partners in ministry.

In making the map, some people begin by naming all the institutions they can recall, and locating them on the map. They find the gas station on the corner, and the bank down the street, the library and the municipal buildings, the school and the recreation park. They begin by putting the particular items in place, and then step back to see the larger picture. Other people want to see the big picture first and then fill in detail. They identify different ways that the land is used by commercial, industrial, agricultural, governmental, and community groups. Which areas are residential? Where are the businesses? In either case, the map should include roughly the same information—who are your institutional neighbors, and where are they located?

Now go back to be sure you have particular groups. Have you identified all the other churches and religious groups? Try to recall from memory; then research for the rest. Mark especially the social agencies that provide resources for the community, including your neighborhood schools, community centers, social security office, police station, courts, and the like. Identify other major institutions in your community, such as large employers, civic and cultural centers, and major gathering places.

Your Church in Community Map can also be made more attractive if you attach photographs of old community buildings and major community events, both recent and from the past. Note especially the vitality in particular religious, social, and cultural centers, such as storefront churches, lodges, pubs, and such.

Finally, do an inventory of your connections with these groups: What are the programs that you have done together? Who among your members are involved with various agencies, employers, and volunteer organizations? List those events, programs, and people as well.

CHAPTER TEN

Resources for Expanding Ministry

A quarter century ago, denominational organizations appeared to be the lifeline for small, struggling mainline churches. Since that time, mainline denominational resources have radically declined, while small churches have stayed about on course. The denominational lifeline has all but disappeared. And it could not have happened at a better time, from the perspective of small church leaders.

At the same time, support for a wide variety of independent churches has increased through seminaries and bible colleges, through publishers and pension programs, and through independent agencies and organizations that specialize in specific areas of ministry. Both the denominations and the independent organizations have provided the same kinds of help: preparation of clergy, leadership training and program materials, consultant service, and financial support.

Help from Denominational Sources

From denominational sources, trained and ordained clergy are the most important resource. The Lord calls the pastor, the congregation feels the call, and, in some cases, the bishop (or his representative) hands it out. But the denomination has a general responsibility for the preparation of the clergy, for the quality of clergy leadership, and for the continuing education of those who have been called. The presence of ordained clergy in good standing signifies a kind of legitimacy to a congregation that small churches still value, more or less, depending on the congregation's commitment to denominational heritage.

The importance of well-prepared clergy is reflected in the percentage of available resources that the small church will spend. Sometimes more than 80 percent of the budget will be devoted to the pastor's compensation. Even more, the small church of fewer than one hundred members will give money far out of proportion to its size if it has the remote hope of securing, as they say, "a pastor of our own" (suggesting a strong sense of ownership). This financial commitment that gives rise to the general belief that small churches give more. They do, if they can reach the necessary income to have a resident, recognized clergy—the symbol of general acceptance. Without that incentive, their financial giving is below average.

Apart from a pastor, denominational resources also include the training and enrichment of the lay leadership of the congregation. State and regional meetings, weekend retreats, summer conferences, Bible camps, special conventions and assemblies all contribute to the preparation and growth of laity as leaders in the local congregation. Such programs allow church membership to share their perceptions of the church, their pride in a Christian history, and their vision of the future for Christian witness. Often overlooked by most members of small churches, these meetings provide a resource of understanding and commitment that brings the denomination together and can strengthen commitment to the local congregation.

Denominational staff and special consultants are also available to local congregations. Most denominations have attempted to locate staff personnel where they are immediately accessible to the needs and interests of local congregations. These staff persons put primary effort into helping members of small churches expand their perspective on their ministry. Perspective is one dimension in which most small churches need assistance. They may know much more about their own situation, but they rarely know how their situation compares with others. Denominational contacts invite the local church to see the larger picture of their ministry.

Denominations can provide information on conditions (issues, resources, pending changes) in the community context for its ministry. By involving members of small churches in conversations about strategies and resources, denominations can learn from the other. In areas of our study, the small congregations actually had more members per capita serving on committees, commissions, and agencies of the judicatory than did the larger congregations. These small-church members gained perspective on local church problems by serving with the judicatory committee. But their insights were often lost to the local congregation, because their representatives were not invited to share their experiences, and the congregation did not know how to use their experience. For the participants, however, it was consoling just to learn that other congregations have problems "just like ours."

In our experience, pastors were expected to participate officially, perhaps too much. Rather, they needed to be drawn into the informal sharing with other clergy, and their spouses. Pastors who began to feel negative about their congregation needed to share their stories with others who have stories of their own. Pastors who confront continually discouraging situations needed supportive friends *outside* the particular setting in which they serve. It is a family problem, and many judicatories discovered that supporting the pastor's spouse was even more important in the low spots of their (shared) ministry. Clergy like their work better when their spouse is happy.

Small church leaders need the affirming insights that only come when they talk with trusted peers about sharing models of specific programs and alternative strategies for changing situations. The farmer-elder who says "we grow more corn and fewer people every year" must know that he is not alone in facing that condition. The congregation that is perpetuating a service no longer needed should be shown how others have reshaped their ministry and redirected their energy. Leaders of the church on the metropolitan fringe, where old-timers are freezing out new families, need to talk with pastors who have lived through it elsewhere. Local congregations need the kind of vision and perspective that denominational conversations are able to provide.

"We don't need more denominational programs," said an elderly officer of a local congregation. "We need contacts with people who have been there, and examples of what they did; and, above all, we need wisdom to help us make decisions." He called this practical wisdom the "missing rung on the ladder" between the denomination and the local congregation. Wisdom, they say, is a good idea that has been refined by experience.

Finally, in the old days, denominational resources included money in cash grants and bank credits. Available funds create an ambivalent relationship between the denomination and the congregation. When the congregation needs financial support, denominations may ask for something in exchange. Often the local church leader called the denomination a combination of Sugar Daddy and Big Brother—they are "sometimes ready, and always watching."

When financial support was available for small congregations, it often came, as one church treasurer pointed out, "to the largest item in our annual budget, the pastor." Throughout mainline churches, the subsidy was provided for the pastor's salary. Even when it is designated "aid to churches," the supplementary funding ceased when the pastor moved to another calling. Funding for the pastor usually involved expectations of growth or particular ministry. Direct funding for the pastor is degrading to the church, and the results are doubtful.[2] Rather, the denominational offices needed a more open and fair procedure.

As in marriage (and most other relationships), decisions on the distribution of money provide the reality test of the values you proclaim. In an effort to be fair and equitable in the distribution of available funds, denominations tried to determine objective bases for funding local churches along with other projects. Although the argument is outdated since most (but not all) of the funding has dried up, it still provides a reality lens—not only for examining small churches, but perhaps more revealing, for understanding the denominational logic that established and maintained these criteria.

The Viable Church

In order to rationalize their investments, denominations try to define "the viable church." *Viable*, a term borrowed from the life sciences, carries a range of connotations, from "barely able to survive" to being "full of life" and ultimately capable of sustained growth." The term is associated with congregations for the purpose of measuring and comparing to determine which ministries should receive support from limited funds. Measures of viability evaluate three dimensions of the situation: the need for that particular witness, the cost to the local church and to the denomination, and the *will or determination* in ministry. Most measures of the viability of a church focus on the will or determination of the congregation to follow through, and usually use one of the following approaches in assessing the *viable commitment* of the congregation.

One approach uses an objective, statistical measurement. This procedure asks not for total figures, but for percentages. For example, it will ask the percent of membership present at an average Sunday worship, the percent of Sundays when the laity assist in worship leadership, the percent of cumulative income of church families that is received in the church budget, the percent of pledging families, and the percent of leadership attendance in denominational meetings. Typically, the standards are high. For example, in one denomination the "viable church" has been set at 50 percent worship attendance, 25 percent lay leadership of worship, 5 percent of family income to the church, 100 percent pledging families, 100 percent attendance at denominational meetings—all criteria considerably above the national averages. Other objective criteria include the use of the denominational hymnbook, denominational Sunday school literature, denominational fund-raising materials, denominational procedures for program planning and evaluation, and the development of a ten-year plan for the congregation. The criteria are objective, and the standards far exceed denominational norms. Surprisingly, many small church leaders find this approach relatively comfortable. They do not measure up, of course. But once they get by that hurdle, as one church officer said, "In percentage participation, we can always hold our own."

A second approach to measuring viability seeks only to determine the regularity of the congregational process. It asks the church to certify the regularity of worship, of Sunday school, of church board meetings, of reports to the church boards, of the administering of the sacraments, of attendance at denominational meetings, of elections for officers. Such a measure is often welcome because it trusts that appropriate programs will result from "regular process." A variation is to ask if the congregation has a "system" for pastoral care, a "process" for planning, a "program" for evangelism, a "plan" for stewardship. This approach avoids the sticky problems of trying to make comparisons of appropriateness and effectiveness among situations that are basically different in regards to location and personnel.

A third approach to viability is based on the mission of the congregation. Commitment is measured on the basis of the accuracy, integrity, or impelling description of the request for funding. Admittedly, the reports accompanying these requests are more exciting to read, and may have a side effect of generating additional resources in the authors (as they convince themselves) and in the readers (as the reports are circulated throughout the judicatory). Some requests emphasize the need, others the resources already available, others the special skills and interests of both pastor and membership. In general, the denominational staff seems more involved in developing these requests and more enthusiastic about their result. The trust level between denominational staff and local personnel seems higher, but usually the congregation was informally selected by denominational staff before the written request was initiated. The mission request may be more stimulating than a statistical viability report, but there is no evidence that it is more accurate in predicting the future of the church.[3]

Each style of measurement examines a different dimension of the small church. The first looks at the hard core of church membership and compares it with others. The second looks at the pace and endurance of the membership to see if it will last for the long haul. The third asks for enthusiasm for a particular task at a particular time with a particular leadership. After great effort has been invested to be fair, equitable, and sensitive to congregational requests, the results are inconclusive. Denominations still cannot determine which congregations are "good investments," and congregations often have the feeling of receiving too much attention—as one member said, "like radishes that are pulled up every few days to see how we are growing."

Some residual tensions remain. Small church leaders are likely to see themselves as fortunate to be part of a "real Christian fellowship" where people are more important than program, and growth is measured in decades and generations. Conversely, leaders of the denomination are apt to view themselves as stewards of the Lord's resources, applying facts and reasons to difficult problems, and using mature management to develop strategies. Perhaps we should recognize the ancient roots of these misperceptions, that each view has merit, which, in practice, appears to misunderstand the others.[4] Even the compliments reflect the tension—for example, the consultant who said, "The small churches always have the best cooks, but they never seem to eat on time or finish eating."

Money Is Not the Problem

Most small churches pay their own way. This is the "secret" of the majority of small congregations that have no denominational affiliation to appeal to, or no expectation of receiving funds to sustain them in a crisis. With meager resources and maximum effort, most small congregations retain their financial independence. In fact, the heartiest small churches are intentionally and aggressively independent; they choose to belong where funds are simply not available. Perhaps they knew from experience what Edward Hassinger discovered in his massive study of small rural churches, that the introduction of denominational procedures, including financial support, reduced the resolve of the congregation to retain its independence.[5]

These independent churches are wonderfully imaginative in creating alternative institutions and loose structures that generate their own income. Even without denominations, they have financially strong networks among publishers[6] with a full range of products from graded educational literature, worship bulletins, and offering envelopes, to music supplies, religious study books, and a large selection of Christian novels. Like the independent churches they serve, these publishers and bookstores operate on free market principles and are far more numerous than denominational outlets, expertly expanding an ever-larger market share. Educational institutions have also evolved to serve this niche market, including Bible schools, seminaries, and universities.[7] Although they seek accreditation through normal procedures, these institutions have been far more willing to develop non-degree programs, offer certificates rather than degrees, provide courses on nights and weekends, and generally be responsive to needs of a more mature clientele who must juggle their education with family and job. Reluctantly, mainline denominational institutions have become more flexible to meet many of the same demands.

Money is not the problem. Independent and denominational small churches need imagination and determination more than financial support. Some have withdrawn into the own meager resources, lived simply, economized, and, as we noted above, survived. Some of these have become little more than family chapels, and even the incentive of additional denominational funding has not stirred them from their reclusive lifestyle. But far more small churches have been able stretch their resources, reach out in love, expand their ministry at a comfortable pace, and feel better about calling themselves "Christian."

Three strategies for expanding ministry seem most pervasive: expand the budget by working with a tentmaker pastor; combine ministries with other congregations; and tap into the amazing world of electronic communities.

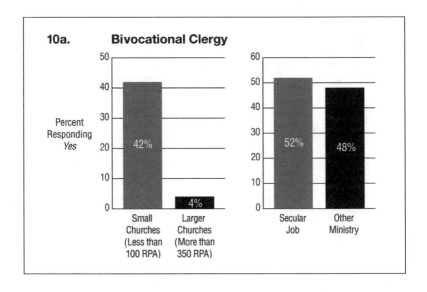

Tentmaking Ministries

Bivocational clergy represent a growing movement in all sorts of smaller congregations, as suggested by FACT data (Fig. 10a).

Quietly, a dramatic change has taken place among mainline clergy who once felt the need for full-time status—now they feel that they are called to be tentmakers.[8] They do not leave the their status as lay members to attend seminary in order to find their ministry. Rather than abandon either sacred or secular employment, at least half of the bivocational clergy simply add to their current responsibilities to fulfill themselves and to extend their calling. This model of the independent, self-sufficient ministry has biblical foundations in the ministry of the apostle Paul (Acts 18:3, 20:34). It has always been strong in independent churches, whose affirmation of the transforming work of the Holy Spirit has an anti-intellectual aspect. In mainline churches, the tentmaker movement was adopted by the worker-priests in the early part of the twentieth century in Europe and later in the United States. Tentmaking was more than an alternate means of financial support. It provided pastors with direct, personal, and continuous contact with the work-world reality of parishioners.

The contemporary tentmakers come from all sorts of backgrounds, labor and management, farmers and teachers, factory workers and social counselors. By any standard, bivocational clergy as a group have spent more years in higher education and hold more advanced degrees than comparable clergy who have a single calling.[9] On the whole, they are a remarkably gifted group of pastors, most of whom felt underemployed with a single vocation.

Three brief comments seem appropriate for those who are interested in further exploration of this option. First, it is far more pervasive than most denominational statistics suggest. Even within the same denomination, identical circumstances might be recorded as "temporary," "auxiliary," "supply," "vacant," or might even escape any special designation at all. Congregations may act unilaterally to make an arrangement with a student, hire a retired cleric, or borrow a pastor from another denomination without reporting to denominational authorities or receiving a response from them. In his epilogue to *Case Histories of Tentmakers*, James Lowery accurately reports, "Mainline denominations simply could not operate in many jurisdictions without the constant support of and use of tentmaking clergy."[10]

We have also discovered that tentmaking relationships are difficult to initiate and almost impossible to transfer from one pastor to the successor. Studies of tentmakers suggest the strength and limits of this movement: far more tentmakers already existed than are recognized by denominational leaders, and yet denominations have a difficult time finding new recruits.[11] Tentmaking would appear to be more natural among independent churches, reflecting an entrepreneurial character of the call that is deeply and personally felt. Mainline denominations might better encourage those who find themselves called to be tentmakers, but not attempt to design an ecclesiastical channel for developing tentmaker clergy.

For mainline churches, tentmaking ministries have proven particularly useful in providing a model for dual assignment contracts within a single denominational structure. The pastor of a small congregation can combine a contract with a parish for part of the time, along with a contract for some other phase of church or judicatory program. These dual contracts are very successful when pastors are also responsible for managing summer camps, developing youth ministries, consulting in Christian education with other congregations, developing ministries of care, or organizing support systems for pastors and spouses. In these dual contracts within the church structure, the pastor has many of the same satisfactions as the tentmaker: he or she feels that his or her professional skills are more fully utilized, and the congregation no longer feels that they are on "ecclesiastical welfare."

For both mainline and independent churches, tentmaking can assume the form of lay leadership for congregations who set aside one of their members to lead them. Although running counter to the push toward professionalism, this form of guiding small churches has two thousand years of history. Lay leadership is still maintained in segments of denominations like the Mennonites and Friends, and is currently experiencing a renaissance among small Christian communities as well.

Cooperative Parish Ministries

FACT research data offers convincing evidence that across our country, congregations have found their way to work together in ministry. (Fig. 10b) A former generation of small-church leaders talked of "Cooperative Parish Ministries" that happened "where

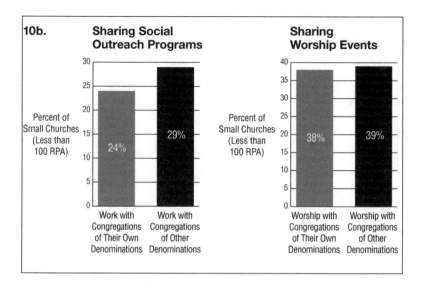

10b.

Sharing Social Outreach Programs

Percent of Small Churches (Less than 100 RPA)

24% — Work with Congregations of Their Own Denominations

29% — Work with Congregations of Other Denominations

Sharing Worship Events

Percent of Small Churches (Less than 100 RPA)

38% — Worship with Congregations of Their Own Denominations

39% — Worship with Congregations of Other Denominations

people of God in different congregations within a given geo-graphic area find a means of ministry to all the people and all the needs of the people within the area."[12] Surprisingly, perhaps, congregations are more likely to work with churches of different denominational backgrounds to support common community ministries. Further, they are significantly more likely to worship together than to share in social ministry (although small churches worship within and beyond their denomination about equally, while larger churches tend to worship with others more often— see FACT Report). Clearly, throughout the nation, congregations have found common grounds in both their work and worship.

Organizational designs and strategies for congregational clusters have taken many forms, which reflect differences in religious heritage, congregational resources, and personalities.[13] One cooperative parish was studied during its three-year trial run.[14] The research project included five congregations that "appeared to have histories typical of congregations located in suburban fringe places . . . did not seem to be attracting new people very well . . . having difficulty with church school, with program for young people, and in holding the quality of pastoral leadership." It focused on the quality of leadership and program, the development of pastoral leadership, and the role of the denomination in supporting the clustering of churches.

In one sense, the project was a resounding success: the programs expanded in quality and variety. More people participated in cluster programs and in separate church events. New people attended, and older members became more active. The pooling of resources gave confidence for more adventuresome efforts, and the ventures proved successful. People came. Pastors felt the momentum pick up. Above all, the pastors enjoyed the new depth of relationship that developed from working together, sharing their concerns, and contributing their own unique gifts of ministry as needed in the common effort. They especially appreciated the organization of a common office in the community around which they worked. Professionally and personally, they became very attached to one another and to the cluster of churches.

But here is the problem: the members of these churches had a very different view of the three-year experience. Their reactions should not surprise anyone who has worked in cooperative parish ministries. The most frequent comment concerned size: "Cluster programs were too big . . . . Size was overwhelming."[15] People had a sense of being lost in the crowd. In commenting on the reaction of one congregation, the analyst summarizes: "The cluster, which tended to break up this close-knit community as people spread their efforts and their activities across a larger group, was a counterproductive experience to people in this highly active, close-knit, small congregation." The caring cell of the church family had been broken. Further, they reported an "issue of pace . . . the increase in activity eventually became a burden." Everything was done right, but "there was so much to do, and it all had to be done so quickly."

Place was also a problem. Members were uncomfortable about the Cooperative Church office, not that they had a new one, but they did not have the old. The pastor was less local and less available than he had been when his office was in the manse. The actual distance was not the issue. Turf was at stake, and they had lost him to a neutral turf. One typical comment reflected a common view: "The tight band between minister and congregation has been broken. Now it's like going to see a businessman." The pastors loved working closely with colleagues, yet experienced some of the same grief in the lost intimacy with the congregation.

Finally, with a jolt, the five church boards voted against continuing the Cooperative Ministry project. They had more money, yes, and more programs to pay for. On balance, they had not seen evidence that the project financially helped or spiritually enriched their churches. More people were participating, but they were not assimilated into the congregations. The report summarizes the dilemma: "New residents and non-members . . . do not have the same traditional ties of family and community roots which encourage participation by long-standing members. Therefore, the cluster, with its high quality programming, is an important attracting point for new members and an important ingredient in bringing the churches toward a fruitful future. . . . On the other hand, preserving a close-knit, supportive congregational life in individual churches is equally important." The leaders in this cluster stumbled because, in my view, they placed a priority on new programs to reach new members without strengthening the single-cell, culture-carrying values so highly prized in small churches.

Partners: Faith-based and Beyond

By contrast, a similar project was organized by clustering the congregations in a struggling town in Appalachia, with far less promise of success.[16] Since they came together in response to the collapse of the community economy and the departure of industries that had provided most of the employment for their region, it would appear that they had less from which to build their ministry. But in Ivanhoe, Virginia, they approached their task with a significantly different emphasis.

- First, the partners were different, and so was the organizational structure in which they worked. In Ivanhoe, the religious leaders created an informal network of local groups that were held together by a common vision for their community. Although based in the churches, the organizers included informal associations and even business leaders, and anyone else who was

willing to roll up their sleeves and join in the recon-
struction.

- Second, the leaders and the location were different.
Laity became strong leaders throughout the project,
supported by clergy, who took their turns as
spokesperson and prime mover. Professional creden-
tials were far less important; competence was measured in the ability to achieve the task. Meeting places
were determined by the task at hand, which moved
from churches to the general store, from the courthouse
to Main Street.

- Third, they were grounded in living room Bible studies
and theological reflection, with a distinctly liberationist
perspective. They challenged members of the community, under God, to take responsibility for their own
destiny. They built on their local traditions and brought
biblical faith to focus on their condition. They converted what had been seen as negative traits into the
strengths for transforming the community. "Traits such
as passivity, stubbornness, hostility, and superstition
should not immediately be seen as 'sins' from which a
community must repent. Often these very qualities
contain the 'seeds of salvation' (or liberation), which
remain hidden from outsider . . . for example . . . the
early religious music of the Appalachian mountains
[that] was laden with themes of salvation through
struggle."[17]

It is a moving story, how they mobilized these resources;
churches and informal associations, lay and professional leaders,
and biblical faith that inverts worldly values and empowers
through suffering—united to enact their faith in ways that
restored confidence and community back into their town. They
literally acted out their struggle with giant puppets in the public
square, rediscovering their own gifts, and having wonderful fun
doing it. It was far more than the former "cooperative ministry"
among churches—it was a community enlivened with the power
of their faith in action.

Finding Your Partners in Ministry

Most communities have similar resources, and probably more resources as Ivanhoe, Virginia had. Review your "Church in Community Map" from exercise 10, and begin to list the assets of your community.[18] Like in Ivanhoe, what other churches might join you in reflective Bible study to imagine what God is calling you to do in your town? Who are the leaders of informal groups (even concerned citizens who share particular issues) that you might invite into your conversation? Who are the leaders in agencies and organizations that share some of your basic values and commitments, such as schools, community centers and health groups? When ministries are faith-based (more so than church-based—limited to churches and church buildings), small churches in all sorts of communities have given solid ground and new vision to clergy associations and church councils, to partnerships with schools, health centers, and even business leaders who care about the turf they share.

Small churches cannot afford to make sudden decisions, or act out of character. But when that character is caring—personal, local, practical, and faith-filled—small churches have provided the catalyst for community change and renewal. With dedication, more than with massive programs, small churches have shown God's love in action. Using an array of existing assets and potential partners, small-church leaders have enacted God's presence in their midst. By their human relations, more than by organizational ties, small churches have built coalitions across theological differences, and they have combined the religious, educational, social, philanthropic, and even governmental groups into a common and clearly religious vision for their communities. Anthony Pappas and Scott Planting provide a guide to small-church community mission based on "understandings, approaches and strategies that work in the small church because they are consistent with the unique nature of small churches."[19] FACT report makes it clear that they are already involved in many significant issues, far more frequently and intensively than could have been predicted by their size and the depth of resources. These ministries provide an amazing profile of small-church commitments. (Fig. 10c)

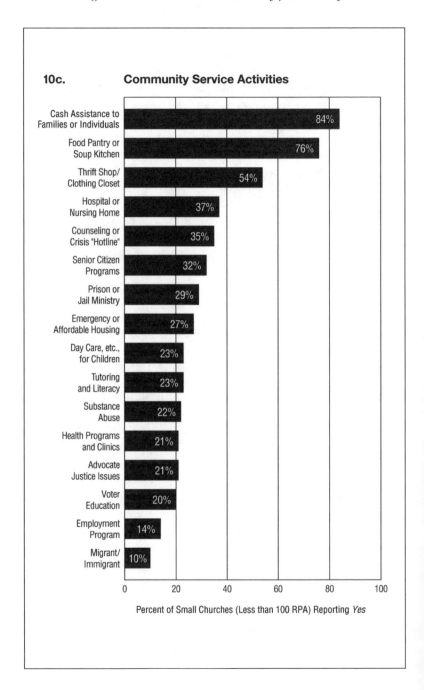

10c. **Community Service Activities**

Activity	Percent
Cash Assistance to Families or Individuals	84%
Food Pantry or Soup Kitchen	76%
Thrift Shop/ Clothing Closet	54%
Hospital or Nursing Home	37%
Counseling or Crisis "Hotline"	35%
Senior Citizen Programs	32%
Prison or Jail Ministry	29%
Emergency or Affordable Housing	27%
Day Care, etc., for Children	23%
Tutoring and Literacy	23%
Substance Abuse	22%
Health Programs and Clinics	21%
Advocate Justice Issues	21%
Voter Education	20%
Employment Program	14%
Migrant/ Immigrant	10%

Percent of Small Churches (Less than 100 RPA) Reporting *Yes*

Visibly Independent, Virtually Connected

"They have so much to offer—why do they keep it to themselves? I can't break through to some of our small churches," complained the denominational program developer in the Midwestern farm belt. His ambivalence reflects the confusion of an outsider looking in at single cell of caring Christians. In the midst of the longest longitudinal study of small, rural churches and their communities, Edward Hassinger maintains that independence of small churches is not an accident:

> The characteristics of local congregations' program may insulate them from the influences of the larger society. Programs tend to be turned inward emphasizing the worship service. . . . The ubiquitous Sunday school is another evidence of self-maintaining, characteristic of the church programs. Sunday schools can be a completely laymen's activity. . . . Resistance to complex organizations was also apparent in the lack of official boards in many churches and the irregularity of their meetings in still more.[20]

By a conservative theology, concentration on caring for members, low overhead on the building cost, and minimum expenses for professional clergy, small churches have maintained their autonomy. The research comments on denominational frustration: "As denominations seek to influence local congregations to conform to their models of program and organization, some congregations may opt out and have the ability to disassociate themselves from the denomination. . . . In reformulating our conception . . . we finally regard congregations as primary groups."[21]

But the twenty-first century offers a radical change that operates unseen well within the local independence of small churches, and yet brings them into conversation with neighbors, resources, and the world. Through email, the Internet, and various forms of telecommunications, some small-church leaders are remaining independent, yet keeping in touch. As seen from National Congregations Study data, smaller churches are investing far out of proportion to their resources and educational levels to keep themselves in touch through e-mail, and to invite others to know about them through the Internet. (Fig. 10d)

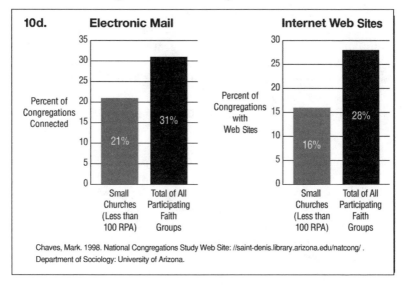

10d.

Electronic Mail

Percent of Congregations Connected

- 21% — Small Churches (Less than 100 RPA)
- 31% — Total of All Participating Faith Groups

Internet Web Sites

Percent of Congregations with Web Sites

- 16% — Small Churches (Less than 100 RPA)
- 28% — Total of All Participating Faith Groups

Chaves, Mark. 1998. National Congregations Study Web Site: //saint-denis.library.arizona.edu/natcong/ . Department of Sociology: University of Arizona.

Unseen in these electronic carriers, small church concerns can be more easily named, friends more easily contacted, consultants more swiftly located, and a wide variety of financial, physical, and even spiritual resources are more readily available. Small churches are investing a disproportionate amount of their slim resources in this form of communication when one in five of the churches gets email, and the number of churches that are in the loop is significantly greater when we include others in the church who use the net informally for personal and professional purposes. In response, numerous resource centers around the world are sharing their experiences and offering quality materials.[22]

These new media technologies can bring the world closer together, making possible new "electronic neighborhoods" and distance learning, reducing the emotional distance and isolation that has plagued many leaders of small congregations in previous generations. The cost would be prohibitive if the church per se were to assume this responsibility. But in small churches, everyone does not need to be computer literate if they can locate a few skilled members (hopefully, including the pastor) who keep in touch. Two factors make a difference—age and employment.

Younger age groups typically have been educated to use the Internet as part of their natural communication patterns, and some jobs have required the use of electronic communication. Not just in urban centers, but in agriculture and other rural industries, going on-line has become a necessity for many church members in their employment and personal lives. Finding a few people willing to go on-line for local churches has not been difficult—they are typically recruited from younger members (or the children and coworkers of older members), some are Internet "addicts and junkies" (avid and well informed). Although these technologies are evolving, literally, with the speed of light, we already see the kinds of contributions that they make to small churches:

- Congregations create instant e-mailing lists that mobilized members to respond to crises or share in celebrations like the old phone trees or "party line" telephones.
- Discussion boards serve like a Sunday school class or fellowship group where members sort out their views, air their grievances, and generally enjoy the current gossip.
- Leaders find resources to deal with a wide variety of needs, evaluate past events, and keep in touch with others in their interest groups or denominational commitments.
- Web sites offer contacts with potential members and build affinity networks that are nurtured by direct and more "personal contact" through email.
- Some small churches have even become educational centers where members come to learn how to use the Internet for personal purposes. One pastor reported a "program in reverse education" where youth teach elderly how to keep in touch with their grandchildren.
- Cyberspace works wonders when the users can distinguish between local contacts and worldwide resources, and avoid getting lost in the wilderness of infinite possibilities.

At the same time, the electronic marvels that can be used to create community can also provide safe space for small-church pastors and leaders to isolate themselves personally while feeling fully in touch by electronic connections. In both the expanded community and the autonomous lifestyle, these forms of electronic communication seem remarkably coherent with small-church psyche. Small churches can remain independent but connected on their time schedule and on their own terms—they decide when to check in, and to whom to respond.

For those small churches that have made the effort, the challenge remains in how to share this information with the rest of the church, how to bring others into the loop. Older pastors, already stretched with existing demands, find it difficult to carve out the time to learn how to use the Internet and time to use it. Personal and congregational habits of communication are, like all habits, difficult to revise or intrude upon. But centers for information, resources and assistance are readily available, and the technology seems amazingly adaptable to allow small churches to have their independence and yet stay as much on the cutting edge as they choose.

Postmodern Challenge

Small churches offer such an attractive image of Christian community that larger congregations often claim to duplicate the experience. They see the small church as creator of relational-wealth, what Robert Putnam has called social capital, and in their small groups they seek to do the same. They say, "Our small groups are a collection of small churches; come and see." Typically, their groups are temporary and task-oriented. But larger churches are not like small churches. Even as "a collection of small churches," the larger church never offers the same feeling as belonging to a small congregation, where everyone is known by name as part of the social fabric. Larger churches should be commended for reaching for such high ideals. They can do many things exceedingly well. But larger churches can never duplicate the single cell of a small Christian congregation.

In fact, they are opposites. In the ways we have described, small churches are counter to large churches and counter to the modern culture that creates the megachurch. Functionally, the small church is intuitively postmodern.[23] Small churches are postmodern in lifestyle and decision making, in their sense of people-time and particular place, in recognition of sacred land and the immanence of God, everywhere. Where large churches emphasize the organization and the spoken word, smaller churches live by relationships, what Tex Sample has called the "oral culture."[24] Where the large church puts a premium on good program and professional leaders, the smaller church will celebrate people and their relationships with leaders and with each other. Where the large church seeks to define issues and plan responses, the small church wants to experience the issues and respond as needed—all postmodern values.

Sometimes, even the small church cannot live up to its own expectations. The small church is a caring cell, or at least it can be. "Caring" challenges the church to be genuinely inclusive. For example, do the pastors and the people really see one another in the choreography of worship, or do they focus on only a few selected people? Are new members really adopted, or do they remain stepchildren with only their Father in heaven and no room to call their own? Is the pastor-as-lover left waiting in the anteroom of important decisions? If church order provides the bones in the body of the Christian continuity, then are some churches more like legalistic skeletons where only the bones of order remain? Christian love can be measured, I believe, by the inclusive quality of the congregation's caring for its own people and place—intuitively a postmodern value.

At the same time, small churches have a theological genius for conservation. They find their identities in past events, their roots in significant places, and their strength in the rhythm of regular events. The quality of their Christian character can be measured by the strength of their positive identity as people who have found a place in God, which can be used for the healing of others in need.

By Gospel standards, churches are challenged to remain effective, not simply to survive. Every congregation should be strong enough to affirm its identity, spiritually and financially. Yet every church should also be sensitive to its need to participate in the larger church—denominational, ecumenical, community networks—as partners in Christian witness. More than working with other churches, our efforts at outreach invite a redefining of old organizational differences between church, school, government and philanthropy. As we have seen above, small congregations in many communities are creating new partnerships of real people who are unashamed of a common religious vision for their communities, and that is postmodern.

A Summary

Small-Church Perspectives

Small churches have restored a basic dimension to the fullness of biblical theology. Small churches have reclaimed the importance of times, events, and history. Small churches have memorialized the significance of people, land, and particular places. Small churches have retained the good vibes, rhythms, seasons, and experiences worth remembering.

In a big world, the small church has remained intimate.
In a fast world, the small church has been steady.
In an expensive world, the small church has remained plain.
In a complex world, the small church has remained simple.
In a rational world, the small church has kept feelings.
In a mobile world, the small church has been an anchor.
In an anonymous world, the small church calls us by name—even by nickname!

As a result, small churches have provided the love of God in even the most difficult conditions.

Small-Church Resources

Small churches have a unique quality of Christian love. They are not always nice; yet they never let go. In a community of high mobility, small churches suffer. As people slow down, small churches offer an alternative way of life. While remaining independent, small churches can stay in touch with each other, and with the soil of the earth. When the national economy experienced a recession, many national companies were forced to delay moving their young executives every three years as expected. This had three interesting effects in one newly constructed suburb that provided the residence for many young management families. First, the moving-van companies were off about 30 percent in their anticipated business. Second, the social counselors and pastors of the community experienced a marked increase in the number of people who had crises in their marriages, apparently related to crises in career advancement. Third, the nurseries that sold plants and bushes noticed a dramatic increase in the sale of trees. For the first time in that new suburb, people began to believe that they would live there long enough to enjoy the shade of their own trees.

Small churches struggle where people keep moving. But there is a place for small churches in a world where people plant their own trees.

Suggestions for Further Reading

Hinsdale, Mary Ann, Helen M. Lewis, and S. Maxine Waller. *It Comes from the People: Community Development and Local Theology.* Philadelphia: Temple University Press, 1995.
Magnificent study and story of small churches together making a big difference.

Missouri School of Religion, Center for Rural Ministry, <www.msr-crm.org>
Bite-sized reports on real issues summarized from a half-century of research.

Pappas, Anthony and Scott Planting. *Mission: The Small Church Reaches Out.* Valley Forge: Judson Press, 1993.
How to get the church into the community and the community into the church.

Schaller, Lyle E. *The Small Church Is Different!* Nashville, Tenn.: Abingdon Press, 1982).
The master of classical wisdom in usable forms.

Notes

Introduction

1. For an overview of this decline, see C. Kirk Hadaway and David A. Roozen, *Rerouting the Protestant Mainstream: Sources of Growth and Opportunies for Change* (Nashville: Abingdon Press, 1995), 19-36.

2. Carl S. Dudley, *Making the Small Church Effective* (Nashville: Abingdon Press, 1978), 22. For current comparison, see chapter 1, endnote 5.

3. FACT includes 14,301 congregations from 41 denominational and faith communities. For the full report, see *Faith Communities Today (FACT) A Report On Religion in the United States Today*, Carl S. Dudley and David A. Roozen (Hartford, Conn.: Hartford Institute for Religion Research, Hartford Seminary, 2001). Regularly Participating Adults (RPA) is the unit of participation that could be used by such a broad coalition of participating groups from Methodists to Muslims, from Mormons to Mennonites.

4. See *Faith Communities Today (FACT) Report.*

5. Albert Borgmann, *Crossing the Postmodern Divide* (Chicago: University of Chicago Press, 1992), 97-102, passim.

Chapter One: Perspectives on the Small Church

1. James L. Lowery, Jr., *Peers, Tents and Owls: Some Solutions to Problems of the Clergy Today* (New York: Morehouse-Barlow, 1973), 89. For an application of church size to program development with study tapes and electronic support (also within the Episcopal framework, and beyond) see Arlin J. Rothauge, *Congregational Vitality* (New York: Episcopal Church Center, 1995).

2. Schaller is the earliest and still most helpful analyst. In Lyle E. Schaller, "Looking at the Small Church: A Frame of Reference," *Christian*

Ministry 8, no. 4 (July 1977): 5: "The most widely used criteria to define the "small" church: (1) number of members, (2) worship attendance, (3) a comparison with past days when the congregation was much larger, (4) the image projected by the pastor's definition of comparative church size, (5) the size of the building, (6) the size of the budget, (7) a full work-load for the minister, (8) an individual's previous experiences in other congregations, (9) the quality of caring relationships among the members, (10) the size, number, and variety of fellowship circles or primary face-to-face groups which together constitute that congregation." Schaller sets the small church in context in *Looking in the Mirror: Self-appraisal in the Local Church* (Nashville: Abingdon Press, 1984).

3. Lyle E. Schaller, "Twenty Questions for Self-evaluation in the Small and Middle Sized Church," *Church Management* (April 1977): 18. Schaller's advocacy for defining church size by worship attendance is reflected in FACT decision to use the standard of Regularly Participating Adults (RPA, see Introduction, above). See also Lyle E. Schaller, *The Small Membership Church: Scenarios for Tomorrow* (Nashville: Abingdon Press, 1994).

4. Schaller's comment in "Twenty Questions for Self-evaluation in the Small and Middle Sized Church," *Church Management* (April 1977) helped churches face the issue, for example, James E. Cushman, *Beyond Survival: Revitalizing the Small Church* (Parsons, W. Va.: McClain Printing Company, 1981) and Steve E. Burt and Hazel Ann Roper, *The Little Church That Could: Raising Small Church Esteem* (Valley Forge, Pa.: Judson Press, 2000).

5. See especially the comparative reports on characteristics of small churches in mainline denominations provided by the Office of Research, General Council on Ministries, The United Methodist Church, 601 West Riverview Ave., Dayton, OH 45406-5543, and the annual reports published by denominational offices such as: Research and Planning, Church of the Nazarene, 6401 The Paseo, Kansas City, MO 64131; Office of Research and Evaluation, Evangelical Luthern Church of America, 8765 West Higgins Road, Chicago, IL 60631; Research Services, Presbyterian Church (U.S.A.), 100 Witherspoon Street, Louisville, KY 40202-1396; Institute of Church Ministry, Seventh-day Adventist Church, Andrews University, Berrien Springs, MI 49104; Office of Research and Evaluation, United Church of Christ, 700 Prospect Avenue, Cleveland, OH 44115; and additional data in Faith Communities Today (FACT), 2001.

6. Large churches are not confined to suburban growth. For example, Mennonite, Lutheran, and Baptist congregations often reach distinctive size in rural areas, while many African Methodist Episcopal and National Baptist churches have grown proportionately in urban areas. See summary report in Faith Communities Today (FACT, 2001), 26, as

compared with reports from particular denominations and data centers such as Historic Black Church Project 2000, Interdenominational Theological Center, 700 Martin Luther King, Jr. Dr., SW, Atlanta, GA 30314.

7. Robert W. Lynn and James W. Fraser, "Images of the Small Church in American History," chap. 1 in *Small Churches Are Beautiful*, ed. Jackson W. Carroll (San Francisco: Harper & Row, 1977), 1-19.

8. Robert Putnam, *Bowling Alone: The Collapse and Revival of American Community* (New York: Simon and Schuster, 2000), 65-79, passim.

Chapter Two: The Caring Cell

1. For more information on Faith Communities Today, FACT Report, and Regularly Participating Adults (RPA) see note 3 to the Introduction.

2. Charles H. Cooley uses this familiar quotation to introduce the concept of the "primary group" in *The Two Major Works of Charles H. Cooley: Social Organization* and *Human Nature and the Social Order* (Glencoe, Ill.: Free Press, 1956), 23. The quotation is preceded by a notation that seems appropriate to a discussion of the small church: "The chief characteristics of a primary group are: a. Face-to-face association, b. The unspecialized character of that association, c. Relative permanence, d. The small number of persons involved, e. The relative intimacy among the participants." Cooley's concept of the primary group is particularly appropriate because of his concern for formation and confirmation of individual values in the context of a variety of intimate group settings: the family foremost, but also the play group, the gang, the school and the neighborhood. It is more limited than the *"community" (Gemeinschaft)* as defined by Ferdinand Tönnies, and more value oriented than the "folk society" discussed by Robert Redfield. For a classic discussion, see Edward A. Shils, "The Study of the Primary Group," in *The Policy Sciences*, eds. Daniel Lerner and Harold D. Lasswell (Stanford: Stanford University Press, 1951), 44-69; for theological use, see Avery Dulles, "The Church as Mystical Communion," *Models of the Church* (Garden City, N. Y.: Doubleday, 1974). See a similar use of small group by Anthony G. Pappas, *Entering the World of the Small Church: A Guide for Leaders* (Washington, D. C.: Alban Institute, 1988), which has been updated and republished as *Entering the World of the Small Church* (Bethesda, Md.: Alban Institute, 2000).

3. For the seminal discussion of this concept see Robert D. Putnum, *Bowling Alone: The Collapse and Revival of American Community* (New York: Simon and Schuster, 2000). For a study of the growing impact of face-to-face experiences in many kinds of small groups, see Robert Wuthnow, *Sharing the Journey: Support Groups for America's New Quest for Community* (New York: Free Press, 1996).

4. Cooley, *Two Major Works*, 23.

5. Theodore H. Erickson, "New Expectations: Denominational Collaboration with Small Churches," chap. 10 in *Small Churches Are Beautiful*, Theodore H. Carroll, ed. (San Francisco: Harper & Row, 1977), 162-63.

6. See Lewis Coser, *The Functions of Social Conflict* (New York: Free Press, 1956), 95, 104-10.

7. See Michael S. Olmsted, *The Small Group* (New York: Random House, 1959).

8. It's always the former owner. One small church leader explained that, "you never get a home with your name until you leave."

9. Robert Ardrey, *The Territorial Imperative* (New York: Laurel, 1966), 217-18. For a sensitive awareness of space in the small church, see David R. Ray, *The Big Small Church Book* (Cleveland: Pilgrim Press, 1992). David Ray has updated his excellent study, published as *The Indispensable Guide for Smaller Churches* (Cleveland: Pilgrim Press, 2002).

10. See Julius Fast, "When Space Is Invaded," chap. 4 in *Body Language* (New York: Evans, 1970), 45-63.

11. In the use of pews and the development of meaningful space, entirely different perspectives are provided by John H. Westerhoff, III and Gwen Kennedy Neville, "Rites and Rituals for a Double World—Private and Public Meanings," chap. 5 in *Generation to Generation: Conversations on Religious Education and Culture* (Philadelphia: Pilgrim Press, 1974), and Thomas Oden, "Repertoire of Intensive Group Strategies," chap. 1 and "Encounter and Celebration," chap. 5 in *The Intensive Group Experience: The New Pietism* (Philadelphia: Westminster Press, 1972). For a more contemporary and appreciative interpretation, see Thomas Edward Frank, *The Soul of the Congregation: An Invitation to Congregational Reflection* (Nashville: Abingdon Press, 2000).

12. For one of the earliest studies of the meaning of space in worship, see Melvin D. Williams, *Community in a Black Pentecostal Church: An Anthropological Study* (Pittsburgh: University of Pittsburgh, 1974). For a more recent and comprehensive view, see Nancy T. Ammerman, Jackson W. Carroll, Carl S. Dudley, William McKinney, eds. *Studying Congregations: A New Handbook* (Nashville: Abingdon Press, 1998.

13. Peter L. Berger, *A Rumor of Angels* (Garden City, N. Y.: Doubleday, 1969), 66.

14. Ibid., 67, 69. See also the integration of a sense of order into the entire life of the small church in David R. Ray, *The Big Small Church Book*.

15. Olmsted, *The Small Group*, 23: "Most primary groups are small . . . but not all small groups are primary." For a more basic discussion of the characteristics of these tensions in the small church, see Carl S. Dudley,

Affectional and Directional Orientations to Faith (Washington, D. C.: Alban Institute, 1982).

16. Milton Mayeroff, *On Caring* (New York: Harper & Row, 1971), 2, 40.

17. The mixture of task and feeling is especially evident in the recent, widespread development of "small Christian communities" that are loosely related to some Roman Catholic parishes. See the case studies and essays in Robert S. Pelton, S.C., ed. *Small Christian Communities: Imaging Future Church* (Notre Dame, Ind.: University of Notre Dame Press, 1997).

Chapter Three: Growth by Adoption

1. See Kurt Lewin, *Resolving Social C[onflicts and Field Theory in Social Science,* (Washington, D. C.: American Psychological Association, 1997) for a discussion field theory in general and gatekeepers in particular. David R. Ray has an excellent review of this approach in *The Big Small Church Book* (Cleveland: Pilgrim Press, 1992).

2. Arthur J. Vidich and Joseph Bensman, *Small Town in Mass Society: Class, Power and Religion in a Rural Community* (Princeton: Princeton University Press, 1968), 251. See also a more appreciative and hopeful approach in Peter J. Surrey, *The Small Town Church* (Nashville: Abingdon, 1981).

3. See David R. Ray, *Small Churches Are the Right Size* (New York: Pilgrim Press, 1982).

4. Lyle E. Schaller, "Looking at the Small Church," *Christian Ministry* 8, no. 4 (July 1977): 7: "Chemists use the term 'supersaturated' to describe a solution in which the concentration of the solid dissolved in that liquid is abnormally high. . . . [The small church] is a 'supersaturated' group, with more members than the normal face-to-face primary group can hold." Schaller takes a much more challenging position in subsequent publications; see Lyle E. Schaller, *The Small Membership Church: Scenarios for Tomorrow* (Nashville, Tenn.: Abingdon Press, 1994).

5. C. Peter Wagner, *Your Church Can Grow* (Ventura, Calif.: Regal Books, 1984), 96-98, 105.

6. Ibid., 123. Church Growth themes for small churches use phrases like "resistant members," "turnaround strategies," and "leadership conversion"; see, for example, C. Wayne Zunkel, *Growing the Small Church: A Guide for Church Members* (Elgin, Ill.: D. C. Cook Pub. Co., 1983) and Gary Exman, *Get Ready—Get Set—Grow! Church Growth for Town and Country Congregations* (Lima, Ohio: C. C. S. Pub. Co., 1987).

7. Allan W. Wicker and Anne Mehler, "Assimilation of New Members in a Large and a Small Church," *Journal of Applied Psychology* 55, no. 2 (1980):151-56.

8. Following Schaller, Church Consultant Dirk Hart tells of a congregation that grew by starting a parallel group called MOP (Mothers of Preschool children) that began with coffee, then reflection, Bible study, and eventually the group began worship that attracted new members. The challenge moved to integration of the two groups into one church, keeping the integrity of each, and still creating something more and different.

9. For a helpful discussion of journey theology, see Tex Sample, *U. S. Lifestyles and Mainline Churches: A Key to Reaching People in the 90's* (Louisville: Westminster/John Knox Press, 1990).

10. See foundational work of Wade Clark Roof, *A Generation of Seekers: The Spiritual Journeys of the Baby Boomer Generation* (New York: Harper Collins, 1993).

11. For a current, comprehensive discussion and several congregational case studies (not focused on church size), see Jackson W. Caroll and Wade Clark Roof, *Bridging Divided Worlds: Generational Cultures in Congregations* (San Francisco: Jossey-Bass, 2002).

12. For a particularly helpful discussion, see Dorothy C. Bass, ed. *Practicing Our Faith: A Way of Life for Searching People* (San Francisco: Jossey-Bass, 1997). Join the continuing conversation at www.practicingourfaith.org. Also see David D. Hall, ed. *Lived Religion in America: Toward a History of Practice* (Princeton, N.J.: Princeton University Press, 1997).

13. See especially William Vitek and Wes Jackson, eds. *Rooted in the Land: Essays on Community and Place* (New Haven, Conn.: Yale University Press, 1996). There are countless hard-to-get publications reflecting these values, such as Joyce Sasse, *The Country Preacher's Notebook: Stories and Meditations Reflecting the Spirit of Rural People* (Pitch Creek, Alberta, Canada: Country Preacher Publications, 1997).

14. Excellent research from denominational perspective has been contributed by Dean R. Hoge, Benton Johnson, and Donald A. Luidens in *Vanishing Boundaries: The Religion of Mainline Protestant Baby Boomers* (Louisville, Ky.: Westminster/John Knox Press, 1994).

15. Theodore H. Erickson, "New Expectations," *Small Churches Are Beautiful,* Jackson W. Carroll, ed. (San Francisco, Harper & Row, 1977), has made a helpful distinction between covenant and contract. A contract consists of specific articles of agreement, is written, and is legally enforceable. A covenant is an agreement to "walk together."

16. Lyle E. Schaller, *Hey, That's Our Church!* (Nashville: Abingdon, 1975), 34-38, 93-96, passim. These themes were helpfully expanded in *The Small Church Is Different!* (Nashville: Abingdon, 1982) and *The Small Church Is Different! Leader's Guide* (Nashville: Abingdon, 1990).

Chapter Four: Pastor/People Tensions

1. Conflict is central to understanding and leading small congregations. Although here we note its unique sources in small churches, we will comment on the uses of conflict in chapter 8.

2. Lyle E. Schaller provides a parallel list in *The Small Church Is Different!* 58-83.

3. See Anthony Pappas, *Money, Motivation, and Mission in the Small Church* (Valley Forge, Pa.: Judson Press, 1989). In the pressures on leaders, here we note the burden of financial constraints; in the next chapter we explore some creative ways churches have generated additional social and financial resources.

4. Arthur J. Vidich and Joseph Bensman, *Small Town, op. cit.,* 233-4.

5. Jackson W. Carroll and James C. Fenhagen, "The Ordained Clergy in Small Congregations," chap. 5 in *Small Churches Are Beautiful* (San Francisco: Harper & Row, 1977), 78. For a more developed view, see Jackson W. Carroll, *As One with Authority: Reflective Leadership in Ministry* (Louisville: Westminster/John Knox Press, 1991).

6. James E. Cushman provides an excellent overview that locates contemporary congregations in an historical context, liberating the pastor of narrow contemporary expectations in *Beyond Survival: Revitalizing the Small Church.* (Parsons, W. Va.: McClain Printing Co., 1981).

7. For a more extended discussion see Douglas Alan Walrath, *Making It Work: Effective Administration in the Small Church* (Valley Forge, Pa.: Judson Press, 1994). Also see Steve Burt and Douglas Alan Walrath, *Activating Leadership in the Small Church: Clergy and Laity Working Together* (Valley Forge, Pa.: Judson Press, 1988).

8. See Julius Fast, "When Space Is Invaded," chap. 4 in *Body Language* (New York: MJF Books, 1992).

9. See Donald P. Smith, *Clergy in the Cross Fire: Coping with Role Conflicts in the Ministry* (Philadelphia: Westminster Press, 1973), especially "Internalized Role Conflicts," chap. 4. By comparison, see more recent work by Steve E. Burt and Hazel Ann Roper, *The Little Church That Could: Raising Small Church Esteem* (Valley Forge, Pa.: Judson Press, 2000), especially "Leadership and Small Church Esteem," chap. 4.

10. See extensive discussion in William A. Gamson, *Power and Discontent* (Homewood, Ill.: Dorsey Press, 1968), on the question of overt power and covert influence. For a similar discussion of leadership among rural Catholic churches, see David G. Andrews, ed. *Ministry in the Small Church* (Kansas City, Mo.: Sheed and Ward, 1988). For a sensitive guide to dealing with these issues, see John Savage, *Listening and Caring Skills in Ministry* (Nashville: Abingdon Press, 1996).

11. Intimacy and distance are a prime concern for Henri J. M. Nouwen, *Creative Ministry* (Garden City, N.Y.: Doubleday, 1971), and James D. Glasse *Putting It Together in the Parish* (Nashville: Abingdon, 1972). See also David S. Young, *Servant Leadership for Church Renewal* (Scottsdale, Pa: Herald Press, 1999).

12. Some pastors' spouses enjoy the stories. Sometimes they even provide an additional source to enrich the stock and contribute to the growing image of the pastor as a "real character." For a further discussion of the pastor's spouse under pressure, see James Allen Sparks, "Criticism and the Minister's Wife," chap. 7 in *Potshots at the Preacher* (Nashville: Abingdon, 1977).

13. For a parallel approach in an evangelical idiom, see Steve R. Bierly, *Help for the Small-Church Pastor: Unlocking the Potential of Your Congregation* (Grand Rapids: Zondervan, 1995).

Chapter Five: Memory and Ministry

1. For more extensive guidelines for developing congregational time lines, see Nancy T. Ammerman et al. *Studying Congregations: A New Handbook* (Nashville: Abingdon Press, 1998).

2. See Michael S. Olmsted, *The Small Group* (New York: Random House, 1959), 53 ff. For Robert Wuthnow's more recent study of resurging small-group movements in our more atomized contemporary culture, see *Sharing the Journey: Support Groups and America's New Quest for Community* (New York: Free Press, 1996).

3. Sometimes the nickname serves to reinforce the position that a person holds in the group, such as the use of the man's last name rather than his first. What would be formality for some is intimacy for others.

4. See Gwen Kennedy Neville, "The Sacred Community—Kin and Congregation in the Transmission of Culture," chap. 3 in *Generation to Generation* (Philadelphia: United Church Press, 1974), 51-71.

5. For a classic discussion of cultural time, see W. Lloyd Warner, *The Family of God* (New Haven, Conn.: Yale University Press, 1961). David Ray has caught this spirit in his discussion, "Caring: 'Look How They Love One Another,' " chap. 7 in *The Big Small Church Book* (Cleveland: Pilgrim Press, 1992).

6. For a longer discussion of challenges and options facing congregations in changing communities, see Carl S. Dudley and Nancy T. Ammerman, *Congregations in Transition: A Guide for Analyzing, Assessing, and Adapting in Changing Communities* (San Francisco: Jossey-Bass, 2002).

7. G. Ernest Wright and Reginald H. Fuller, *The Book of the Acts of God* (Garden City, N. Y.: Doubleday, 1960), 9.

8. G. Ernest Wright, *The God Who Acts* (Chicago: Henry Regnery Co., 1952), 18-24, 33-58, passim.

9. Wright and Fuller, *The Book of the Acts of God,* 15.

10. Wright, *God Who Acts,* 13. For an even stronger contemporary expression of this view, see Dorothy C. Bass and Craig Dykstra, "Growing in the Practices of Faith," chap. 14 in Dorothy C. Bass, ed. *Practicing Our Faith* (San Francisco: Jossey-Bass, 1997).

11. Lyle E. Schaller, *Survival Tactics in the Parish* (Nashville: Abingdon, 1977), 137.

12. See Max Thurian, *The Eucharistic Memorial* (Richmond: John Knox Press, 1961), especially vol. 1, chap. 2, and vol. 2, chap. 1. As an introduction to excellent work in small church worship, see Linda Osborn, *Good Liturgy, Small Parishes* (Chicago: Liturgy Training Publications, 1996).

13. Wright and Fuller, *Acts of God,* 259. For a classic in congregational studies that uses this theme as its primary insight, see James F. Hopewell, *Congregation: Stories and Structures* (Philadelphia: Fortress Press, 1987). For an excellent recasting of these themes in a postmodern idiom, see Philip D. Kenneson, *Life on the Vine: Cultivating the Fruit of the Spirit in Christian Community* (Downers Grove, Ill.: InterVarsity Press, 1999).

14. James P. Wind, *Places of Worship: Exploring Their History* (Nashville: American Association for State and Local History, 1990), 115. Also see James P. Wind, *Constructing Your Congregation's Story* (Minneapolis: Augsburg Fortress, 1993).

15. For example, see David R. Ray, *Wonderful Worship in Smaller Churches* (Cleveland: Pilgrim Press, 2000).

16. Roy M. Oswald, *Discerning Your Congregation's Future: A Strategic and Spiritual Approach* (Bethesda, Md.: Alban Institute, 1996), 64.

17. For a practical application of this approach, see Steve Burt, *Activating Leadership in the Small Church: Clergy and Laity Working Together* (Valley Forge, Pa.: Judson Press, 1988).

18. Anthony Pappas, *Money, Motivation, and Mission in the Small Church* (Valley Forge, Pa.: Judson Press, 1989), 56.

19. See Herbert Anderson and Edward Foley, *Mighty Stories, Dangerous Rituals: Weaving Together the Human and the Divine* (San Francisco: Jossey-Bass, 1998).

Chapter Six: Places of Ministry

1. Walter Brueggemann, *The Land: Place as Gift, Promise, and Challenge in Biblical Faith* (Philadelphia: Fortress Press, 2002), 5.

2. For an exploration of this common feeling, see Tony Hiss, *The Experience of Place* (New York: Knopf, 1990).

3. Paul Tournier, *A Place for You: Psychology and Religion* (New York: Harper & Row, 1968), 45-46.

4. Brueggemann, *The Land*, 187.

5. Tournier, *A Place for You*, 79.

6. A classic discussion of the importance of place has been provided by Lyle E. Schaller, "Human Ethology: The Most Neglected Factor in Church Planning" *Review of Religious Research* 17, no. 1 (1975): 2-14.

7. To assist congregations in weaving their location with memory, see James P. Wind, *Places of Worship: Exploring Their History* (Nashville: American Association for State and Local History, 1990). Also see James P. Wind, *Constructing Your Congregation's Story* (Minneapolis: Augsburg Fortress, 1993).

8. See especially Tony Hiss, *The Experience of Place* (New York: Knopf, 1990), 144-77.

9. See Tex Sample, *U.S. Lifestyles and Mainline Religion: A Key to Reaching People in the 90's* (Louisville: Westminster/John Knox Press, 1990).

10. Excellent models for small churches can be found in: Laurent A. Parks Daloz, et al. *Common Fire: Leading Lives of Commitment in a Complex World* (Boston: Beacon Press, 1996); Gary Gunderson, *Deeply Woven Roots: Improving the Quality of Life in Your Community* (Minneapolis: Fortress Press, 1997); and Philip D. Kenneson, *Life on the Vine: Cultivating the Fruit of the Spirit in Christian Community* (Downers Grove, Ill.: InterVarsity Press, 1999).

11. V. Elaine Strawn and Christine L. Nees, *Fifteen Services for Small Churches* (Nashville: Abingdon Press, 1992). Also see Anthony G. Pappas, *Mustard Seeds: Devotions for Small Church People* (Columbus, Ga.: Brentwood Christian Press, 1994), now available through Anthony G. Pappas, 69 Weymouth Street, Providence, RI 02906. Phone and fax (401) 861-9405.

12. David R. Ray, *Wonderful Worship in Smaller Churches* (Cleveland: Pilgrim Press, 2000). For similar material from a Catholic perspective, see Linda Osborn, *Good Liturgy, Small Parishes* (Chicago: Liturgy Training Publications, 1996).

13. The summary is found in Max Thurian, "The Memorial as a Liturgical Form," vol. 1, chap. 2 in *The Eucharistic Memorial* (Richmond: John Knox Press, 1961), 20-26.

Chapter Seven: Events Worth Remembering

1. W. Lloyd Warner, *The Family of God: A Symbolic Study of Christian Life in America* (New Haven, Conn.: Yale University Press, 1961), 383. See also Ron Klassen and John Koessler, "Bridging the Cultural Gap," in *No Little Places* (Grand Rapids, Mich.: Baker Books, 1996).

2. John H. Westerhoff, III and Gwen Kennedy Neville, *Generation to Generation* (Philadelphia: United Church Press, 1974), 96-97.

3. Ibid., 97. See also fig. 1, "Institutional Cycles in American Society," ibid., 99.

4. Warner, *Family of God*, 357. For a review of pastoral ministry that appreciates the dramatic quality of these events, see Herbert Anderson and Edward Foley, *Mighty Stories, Dangerous Rituals: Weaving Together the Human and the Divine* (San Francisco: Jossey-Bass, 1998).

5. Westerhoff and Neville, *Generation to Generation*, 83.

6. For an especially creative use of the calendar events, see William H. Willimon and Robert L. Wilson, *Preaching and Worship in the Small Church* (Nashville: Abingdon Press, 1980).

7. Westerhoff and Neville, *Generation to Generation, op. cit.*, 98. Nancy T. Foltz expands this point with a special sensitivity to the rituals that sustain such events in *Caring for the Small Church: Insights from Women in Ministry* (Valley Forge, Pa.: Judson Press, 1994).

8. Warner, *Family of God*, 363.

9. See Westerhoff and Neville, *Generation to Generation*, 62-64.

10. See Gail Sheehy, *Passages—Predictable Crises of Adult Life* (New York: Dutton, 1976). Gail Sheehy raises all the same questions of rites of passage, but her models are mobile, middle-class, management Americans—no elderly, no blue-collar families, and no church or other support communities. Compare her perceptions with those of Westerhoff and Neville, "Life Cycle and Ceremonial Events," fig. 2 in *Generation to Generation*, 104-5.

11. For the centrality of food in such events, see Russell Chandler, *Feeding the Flock: Restaurants and Churches You'd Stand in Line For* (Bethesda, Md.: Alban Institute, 1998). For the importance of food in cross cultural caring, see Carl S. Dudley and Nancy T. Ammerman, *Congregations in Transition: A Guide for Analyzing, Assessing, and Adapting in Changing Communities* (San Francisco: Jossey-Bass, 2002), 157-161.

12. Warner, *Family of God*, 75.

13. Westerhoff and Neville, *Generation to Generation*, 68.

14. Ibid., 44.

15. Donald L. Griggs and Judy McKay Walther, *Christian Education in the Small Church* (Valley Forge, Pa.: Judson Press, 1988), 15.

16. See essays by seasoned practitioners, Nancy T. Foltz, ed. *Religious Education in the Small Church* (Birmingham, Ala.: Religious Education Press, 1990), and the emphasis on education as embodied faith offered by Dorothy C. Bass and Don C. Richter, eds. *Way to Live: Christian Practices for Teens* (Nashville: Upper Room Books, 2002).

17. See program suggestions by Rick Chromey in *Youth Ministry in Small Churches* (Loveland, Colo.: Group Publishing, 1990) and *Children's*

Ministry Guide for Smaller Churches (Loveland, Colo.: Group Publishing, 1995).

18. Mircea Eliade, *The Sacred and the Profane: The Nature of Religion* (New York: Harcourt Brace and World, 1959), 63.

Chapter Eight: Goals, Conflicts, and Renewal

1. For a helpful discussion of this leadership style, see David R. Ray, "Maintenance: Keeping the Ship Afloat and on Course," chap. 9 in *The Big Small Church Book* (Cleveland: Pilgrim Press, 1992), 139-69.

2. Max Weber, "Legitimate Order and Types of Authority," in *Theories of Society: Foundations of Modern Sociological Theory* Talcott Parsons, ed. (New York: Free Press, 1961), 1:229-35.

3. James D. Anderson and Ezra Earl Jones, *The Management of Ministry* (San Francisco: Harper & Row, 1978), pp. 97ff.

4. Urban T. Holmes, III, *The Priest in Community: Exploring the Roots of Ministry* (New York: Seabury Press, 1978), 79. Also see Urban T. Holmes, III, *Spirituality for Ministry* (Harrisburg, Pa.: Morehouse Pub., 2002).

5. Lewis A. Coser, *The Functions of Social Conflict* (Glencoe, Ill.: Free Press, 1956), 31. See also Hugh F. Halverstadt, *Managing Church Conflict* (Louisville: Westminster/John Knox Press, 1991).

6. Coser, *Social Conflict*, 85. See also Speed B. Leas, *Leadership and Conflict* (Nashville: Abingdon Press, 1982) and Edwin H. Freedman, *Generation to Generation: Family Process in Church and Synagogue* (New York: Gilford Press, 1985).

7. Coser, *Social Conflict*, 106. See especially "Propositon 11: The Search for Enemies," chap. 5, 104-10. Also see: John M. Miller, *The Contentious Community: Constructive Conflict in the Church* (Philadelphia: Westminster Press, 1978); Larry L. McSwain and William C. Tredwell, Jr., *Conflict Ministry in the Church* (Nashville: Broadman Press, 1981); G. Lloyd Rediger, *Clergy Killers: Guidance for Pastors and Congregations Under Attack* (Louisville: Westminster/John Knox Press, 1997).

8. See Peter M. Senge, *The Fifth Discipline: The Art and Practice of the Learning Organization* (New York: Doubleday/Currency, 1990). *Fifth Discipline Fieldbook* (New York: Doubleday/Currency, 1995).

9. Ronald A. Heifetz, *Leadership without Easy Answers* (Cambridge, Mass.: Belknap Press of Harvard University Press, 1994).

10. For this approach to clergy leaders, see Jackson W. Carroll, *As One With Authority: Reflective Leadership in Ministry* (Louisville: Westminster/John Knox Press, 1991). For his discussion on post-traditional society, see Jackson W. Carroll, *Mainline to the Future: Congregations for the 21st Century* (Louisville: Westminster/John Knox Press, 2000).

11. With a forward by Anthony G. Pappas, Alice Mann offers resources for renewal that can mobilize the energies of most small churches, *Can Our Church Live? Redeveloping Congregations in Decline* (Bethesda, Md.: Alban Institute, 1999). With encouragement from Herb Miller, Ron Crandall offers a more challenging approach, *Turnaround Strategies for the Small Church* (Nashville: Abingdon Press, 1995).

12. See Dorothy C. Bass, "Keeping Sabbath," chap. 6 in *Practicing Our Faith*, Dorothy C. Bass, ed. (San Francisco: Jossey-Bass, 1997), 75-90.

13. See Amy Plantinga Pauw, "Dying Well," chap. 12 in *Practicing Our Faith, op cit.*, 163-178.

Chapter Nine: Energizing from Within

1. For more information on developing and utilizing congregational maps, see Nancy T. Ammerman et al. *Studying Congregations: A New Handbook* (Nashville: Abingdon Press, 1998). For significant assistance in information gathering, the congregation may secure community information by contacting a local source (municipal planning office, county extension service, university sociology department) or by working through national organizations such as Visions-Decisions, based in Atlanta, and Percept (http://www.perceptnet.com/pn4/address.htm). Although these sources can provide additional information, only your committee can make the maps and bring the study to life for your congregation.

2. See H. Richard Niebuhr, *The Social Sources of Denominationalism* (NewYork: Meridian, 1957) and H. Richard Niebuhr, *Christ and Culture* (London: Faber and Faber, 1952). For a contrast with our contemporary complexity, see R. Stephen Warner and Judith G. Wittner, eds., *Gatherings in Diaspora: Religious Communities and the New Immigration* (Philadelphia: Temple University Press, 1998).

3. See Avery Dulles, *Models of the Church* (Garden City, N.Y.: Doubleday, 1974).

4. For an especially sensitive study of an independent religious approach, see Nancy T. Ammerman, *Bible Believers: Fundamentalists in a Modern World* (New Brunswick, N. J.: Rutgers University Press, 1987). Their evangelical zeal may be seen in perspective of other traditions in David A. Roozen et al. *Varieties of Christian Presence: Mission in Public Life* (New York: Pilgrim Press, 1984).

5. Robert D. Dale, *To Dream Again* (Nashville: Broadman Press, 1981). Also see John R. Kimberly et al., *The Organzational Life Cycle* (San Francisco: Jossey-Bass, 1980), 14, passim. The life cycle concept was first published by Max Weber in 1924 and translated as "The Routinization of Charisma" in 1947, *Theories of Society*, Talcott Parsons, ed. (New York: Free Press, 1961), pp. 1297-1304.

6. See Win Arn, *Five States in the Life Cycle of Churches* (Pasadena, Calif.: American Church Growth, 1985); Martin F. Saarinen, *The Life Cycle of a Congregation* (Washington, D.C.: Alban Institute, 1998); Arlin J. Rothauge, *The Life Cycle in Congregations: A Process of Natural Creation and an Opportunity for New Creation* (New York: Episcopal Church Center, 1995).

7. For example, Neil Harper, *Urban Churches, Vital Signs: Beyond Charity Toward Justice* (Grand Rapids: Wm. B. Eerdmans Pub., 1999); Ron Klassen and John Koessler, *No Little Places: The Untapped Potential of the Small-Town Church* (Grand Rapids: Baker Books, 1996); Bernard Quinn, *The Small Rural Parish* (Washington, D. C.: Glenmary Research Center, 1980); Eldein Villafane, *Seek the Peace of the City: Reflections on Urban Ministry* (Grand Rapids: Wm. B. Eerdmans, 1995); Paul Wilkes, *Excellent Protestant Congregations: The Guide to Best Places and Practices* (Louisville: Westminster/John Knox, 2001); and Paul Wilkes, *Excellent Catholic Parishes: The Guide to Best Places and Practices* (New York: Paulist Press, 2001).

8. Douglas Walrath, "Types of Small Congregations and Their Implications for Planning," chap. 3 in *Small Churches Are Beautiful,* Jackson W. Carroll, ed. (New York: Harper, 1977), 33-61.

9. For adaptive exercises and additional resources, see Carl S. Dudley and Nancy T. Ammerman, *Congregations in Transition: A Guide for Analyzing, Assessing, and Adapting in Changing Communities* (San Francisco: Jossey-Bass, 2002).

10. Lyle E. Schaller, *Parish Planning: How to Get Things Done in Your Church* (Nashville: Abingdon Press, 1971), 167-68.

11. Five parallel church images are adapted from the research and case studies more extensively reported in Carl S. Dudley and Sally A. Johnson, *Energizing the Congregation: Images that Shape Your Church's Ministry* (Louisville: Westminster/John Knox, 1993). These models are also summarized in Carl S. Dudley, *Community Ministry: New Challenges, Proven Steps to Faith-based Initiatives* (Bethesda, Md.: Alban Institute, 2002).

12. *Community Ministry* (Bethesda, Md.: Alban Institute, 2002). The same source informs five parallel models, except the intentional church.

13. Dan Baumann published a delightful case study book of several evangelical, high-commitment churches: *All Originality Makes a Dull Church* (Santa Anna, Calif.: Vision House Publishers, 1976). Michael A. Cowan and Bernard J. Lee have described the close connection between intentional churches and prophetic churches in *Conversation, Risk, and Conversion: The Inner and Public Life of Small Christian Communities* (Maryknoll, N.Y.: Orbis Books, 1997).

14. Intentional churches have been strongly advocated by Protestant theologians such as Stanley Hauerwas and William H. Willimon, *Resident*

Aliens: Life in the Christian Colony (Nashville: Abingdon Press, 1989) and *Where Resident Aliens Live: Exercises for Christian Practice* (Nashville: Abingdon Press; 1996). However the movement is more evident and articulate among Catholics; see Robert S. Pelton, ed., *Small Christian Communities: Imagining Future Church* (Notre Dame, Ind.: University of Notre Dame Press, 1997) and Bernard J. Lee with William V. D'Antonio and Virgilio Elizondo, *The Catholic Experience of Small Christian Communities* (New York: Paulist Press, 2000).

15. Andrew M. Greeley, *Why Can't They Be Like Us? America's White Ethnic Groups* (New York: E. P. Dutton, 1971).

16. For an extended discussion of strategies for using congregational time line, stories, maps, and historical objects, see Carl S. Dudley and Douglas Alan Walrath, *Developing Your Small Church's Potential* (Valley Forge, Pa.: Judson Press, 1988).

17. See Edward P. Wimberly, *Recalling Our Own Stories: Spiritual Renewal for Religious Caregivers* (San Francisco: Jossey-Bass, 1997). Also, Herbert Anderson and Edward Foley, *Mighty Stories, Dangerous Rituals: Weaving Together the Human and the Divine* (San Francisco: Jossey-Bass, 1998).

18. Data for this table comes from the earlier book, *Making the Small Church Effective,* but there seems no reason to believe that these groups have subsequently changed their behavior.

19. For the initial discussion of these data, see Carl S. Dudley, *Making the Small Church Effective* (Nashville: Abingdon Press, 1978), 155-56.

Chapter Ten: Resources for Expanding Ministry

1. For more information on developing and utilizing congregational maps, see Nancy T. Ammerman, et al. *Studying Congregations: A New Handbook* (Nashville: Abingdon Press, 1998).

2. See the discussion in Paul Madsen, *The Small Church—Vital, Valid and Victorious* (Valley Forge, Pa.: Judson Press, 1975), 116 ff.

3. Final report by David J. Brown, Robert Haskins, and William Swisher, *Small Church Project* (New York: United Church Board for Homeland Ministries, June, 1977), 35: "We need to recognize that current staff functions are failing to produce acceptable relationships with local pastors and local congregations. . . . Most congregations are not being strengthened and . . . current staff styles are not aiding them. . . . Churches do not necessarily want professionals, they want friends with professional skills. . . . They want competent people who feel their needs, understand their dreams and share with them in seeking ways to realize their potential. . . . It is not so much what we do that frees congregations but who we are in relation to them. The key to change in local congrega-

tions is the intentional development of loving relationships among staff, pastors, congregations and their leaders."

4. Coser suggests that the "evocation of an outer enemy or the invention of such an enemy strengthens social cohesion that is threatened from within." Lewis Coser, *The Functions of Social Conflict* (New York: Free Press, 1956), 110.

5. Edward W. Hassinger, Jr., Kenneth Benson, James H. Dorsett, and John S. Holik, *A Comparison of Rural Churches and Ministers in Missouri Over a 15-year Period* (Columbia, Mo.: College of Agriculture, 1973). Missouri Rural Church Project is a longitudinal study of approximately 500 congregations that were surveyed in 1952, 1967,1982, and 1998-99 by the Department of Rural Sociology, University of Missouri-Columbia.

6. For example, *The Christian Standard*, Standard Publishing, Cincinnati, Ohio.

7. For example, Abiline Christian University, Abiline, Tex.

8. "No less than 22% of pastors, more than one of every five, engages in secular employment in addition to their parish ministry, according to Robert L. Bonn's study for the National Council of Churches, reported in "Moonlighting Clergy," *Christian Ministry* (September 1975): 110. See "Return of Dual Role Clergy," *The Five Small Stones: A Newsletter for Small Churches* 18, no. 1-3, 2000.

9. "Moonlighting Clergy." See also Robert L. Bonn and Ruth T. Doyle, "Secularly Employed Clergymen: A Study in Occupational Role Recomposition," *Journal for the Scientific Study of Religion* (September 1974). For a similar, more recent study, see L. Ronald Brushwyler, "Bi-Vocational Pastors: A Research Report" (Chicago: Midwest Ministry Development Service, 1992).

10. James L. Lowery, Jr., *Case Histories of Tentmakers* (New York: Morehouse-Barlow, 1976). See current conversation among tentmakers, *www.tentmakersym.org/web/identity.html*.

11. Clergy Occupational Development and Employment (CODE), Rochester, New York, 1975, included: American Baptist, United Church of Christ, and United Presbyterian Church. For a later summary, see also Lyle E. Schaller, "Staffing the Small Church," *The Small Church Is Different!* (Nashville: Abingdon Press, 1982).

12. Marvin T. Judy, *The Parish Development Process* (Nashville: Abingdon Press, 1973), 29.

13. Clusters Guidelines for the Development of Local Church Clusters (Published jointly by the Board of National Missions, UPCUSA, and the Board for Homeland Ministries, UCC, May, 1970). *Strengthening the Small Church for Its Mission.* A Report of the Task Force on Ministry to the Small Church to the 113th General Assembly, Presbyterian Church, U.S. *Special Report.—The Small Church.* Published by Synod of the Lakes and Prairies,

Office of Communication, 8012 Cedar Avenue South, Bloomington, MN 55420. Thomas E. Sykes, *Field of Churches: A Viable Option* (Atlanta: Home Mission Board, SBC, 1989). Joe McNeal, *Models of Multi-Point and/or Cooperative Ministry* (Columbia, Mo: Center for Rural Church Leadership, 2001).

14. Report of the New Scotland Pilot Cluster, Synod of Albany, Reformed Church in America, 1974.

15. Ibid., 5-10. Quotations throughout are taken from the summary.

16. Mary Ann Hinsdale, Helen M. Lewis, and W. Maxine Waller, *It Comes from the People: Community Development and Local Theology* (Philadelphia: Temple University Press, 1995).

17. Ibid., 211.

18. J. P. Kretzmann and John L. McKnight, *Building Communities from the Inside Out: A Path Toward Finding and Mobilizing a Community's Assets* (Evanston, Ill.: Northwestern University Press, 1993.)

19. Anthony Pappas and Scott Planting, *Mission: The Small Church Reaches Out* (Valley Forge, Pa.: Judson Press, 1993). To use this approach as an arena for ministry with young people, see Michael Warden, *Small Church Youth Ministry Programing Ideas* (Love, Colo.: Group Publishing Co., 1994).

20. Edward W. Hassinger, Jr., Kenneth Benson, James H. Dorsett, and John S. Holik, *The Church in Rural Missouri*, 1967. Missouri Rural Church Project is a longitudinal study of approximately 500 congregations were surveyed in 1952, 1967, 1982, and 1998–99 by the Department of Rural Sociology, University of Missouri-Columbia.

21. Ibid. In a prophetic mode, Hassinger observed: "It is hazardous to predict the future of the [small] church but its tenacity in a changing society suggests that another survey in a decade would find the bulk of the congregations operating at the same stand and in about the same level of activity. They will continue to be essentially fellowship groups engaged in internal activities and a frustration for denominational executives."

22. For examples, see:

- Alban Institute and the Indianapolis Center for Congregations, www.congregationalresources.org
- Hartford Institute for Religion Research, www.FACT.hartsem.edu
- Hinton Rural Life Center, www.hintoncenter.org
- Alternative Models for Rural Ministry, Toronto, www.toronto.anglican.ca/leader/Heading290a
- Center for Ministry in Small Churches, Episcopal, www.sewanee.edu/Theology/cmsc/index.htm
- Center for Rural Ministry, Missouri School of Religion, www.msrcrm.org

- Center for Theology and Land, Dubuque, www.wartburgseminary. edu/programs/ctl.htm
- Heartland Network for Town & Rural Ministries, www.seorf.ohiou. edu/~xx042/hide/heart1.html
- National Catholic Rural Life Conference, www.ncrlc.com
- Rural Evangelism Network, United Kingdom, www.users. zetnet.co.uk/bosborne/ren.htm
- Rural Ministry Resource Page, Australia, http://users.netconnect. com.au/~billclrk/
- Rural Ministry Resources & Networking, ELCA, www.elca.org/ do/ruralministry.html
- The Small Church, United Methodist, www.smallchurch.net
- Texas Rural Church Network/Rural Social Science Education, Texas A & M University, www.texasruralchurchnetwork.org
- United Methodist Rural Fellowship (UMRF), www.seorf.ohiou.edu/ ~xx042/hide/urmf.html

23. See David Harvey, "Fordist Modernism vs. Flexible Postmodernism, or an Interpretation of Opposed Tendencies in Capitalism as a Whole," *The Condition of Postmodernity: An Inquiry into the Origins of Cultural Change* (Cambridge, Mass.: Basil Blackwell, 1989), 337-55; also see Albert Borgmann, *Crossing the Postmodern Divide* (Chicago: University of Chicago Press, 1992). For an overview of postmodern theological arguments, see Stanley J. Grenz, *A Primer on Postmodernism* (Grand Rapids: Wm. B. Eerdmans, 1996). For biblical theology, see Walter Brueggeman, *Texts Under Negotiation: The Bible and Postmodern Imagination* (Minneapolis: Fortress Press, 1993). For educational material, see *Tomorrow Is Another Country,* Board of Education (London: General Synod of the Church of England, 1996).

24. Tex Sample, *Ministry in an Oral Culture: Living with Will Rogers, Uncle Remus, and Minnie Pearl* (Louisville: Westminster/John Knox Press, 1994).

Index